THE**VEGETARIAN**COOKBOOK

THE**VEGETARIAN**COOKBOOK

consultant editor
NICOLA GRAIMES

p

This is a Parragon Publishing Book

First published in 2005

Parragon Publishing

Queen Street House

4 Queen Street

Bath BA1 1HE, UK

ISBN: 1-40545-168-8

Printed in China

Created and produced by The Bridgewater Book Company Ltd

Project editor: Sarah Doughty

Project designer: Anna Hunter-Downing

Commissioned photography: Clive Bozzard-Hill

Notes for the reader

This book uses imperial, metric, or US cup measurements. Follow the same units of measurement throughout; do not mix imperial and metric. All spoon measurements are level: teaspoons are assumed to be 5 ml, and tablespoons are assumed to be 15 ml. Unless otherwise stated, milk is assumed to be whole, eggs and individual vegetables such as potatoes are medium and pepper is freshly ground black pepper. Recipes using raw or very lightly cooked eggs should be avoided by infants, the elderly, pregnant women, convalescents, and anyone suffering from an illness. The times given are an approximate guide only. Preparation times differ according to the techniques used by different people and the cooking times may also vary from those given. Optional ingredients, variations, or serving suggestions have not been included in the calculations.

Picture acknowledgments

The Bridgewater Book Company would like to thank the following for permission to reproduce copyright material:
Corbis pp. 11, 45, 168 and front cover.

CONTENTS

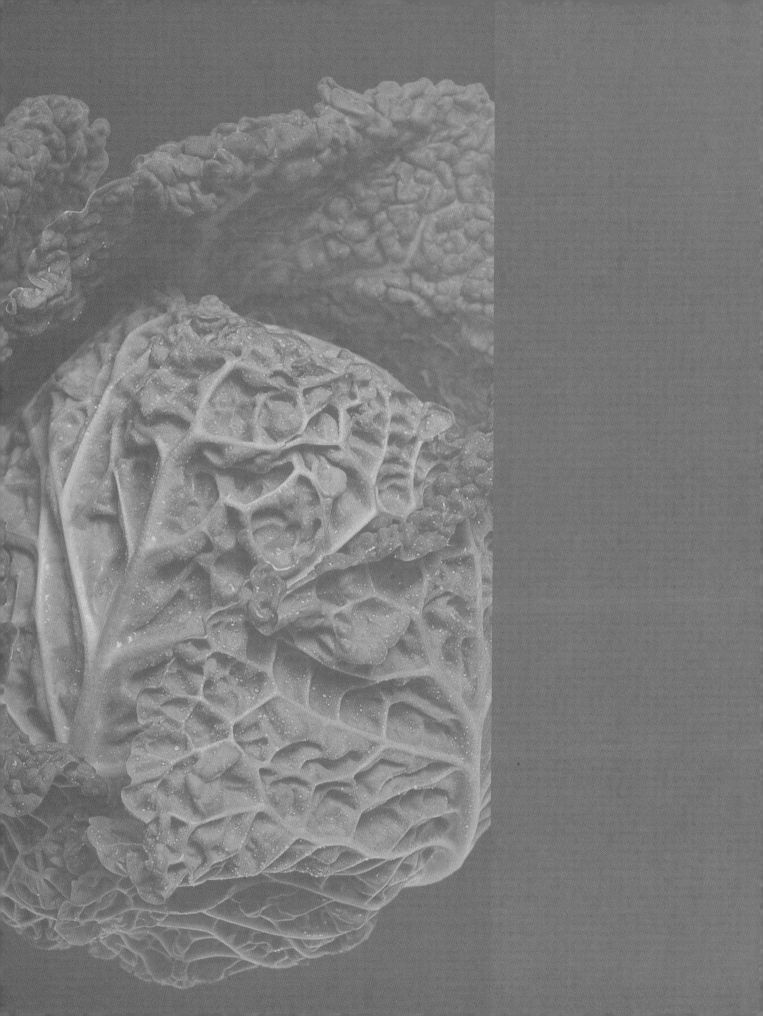

1

The Vegetarian Cookbook is a comprehensive reference book that will help you prepare and enjoy healthy vegetarian meals. Whether you are new to vegetarianism, looking for renewed inspiration, or you simply want to cut down the amount of meat in your diet, you will find lots of new ideas for recipes and ways of cooking vegetarian meals.

INTRODUCTION

Vegetables are, of course, at the heart of a vegetarian diet. There is a huge variety of delicious vegetables to choose from, all full of goodness and nutrients. Eating a balanced diet, which also includes fruit, eggs, dairy, nuts, seeds, lentils, and pulses, is very important and can be achieved by careful planning and combining of foods. The recipes in this book will whet your appetite for healthy vegetarian living, and provide dishes that are ideal for every occasion.

What is a Vegetarian?

A vegetarian is someone who chooses not to eat meat, poultry, fish, or byproducts of meat and fish, such as gelatin. Lacto-ovo-vegetarians include eggs and dairy products in their diet, while lacto-vegetarians avoid eggs. Vegetarians who avoid dairy products and eggs, and nonfood items produced from animals are known as vegans.

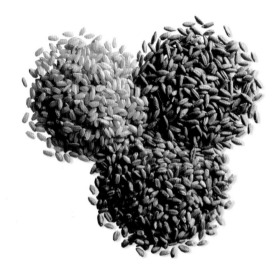

WHY BE VEGETARIAN?

There are many reasons for becoming vegetarian. Some people give up meat and fish because they do not approve morally of killing animals, or because they are unhappy with ways in which animals are kept or killed for food. Some are concerned about the effect that keeping livestock for meat is having on land that could otherwise be used for growing crops, as well as for environmental reasons. Many people are also becoming vegetarian because of the health benefits it can offer them.

WHAT ARE THE BENEFITS?

Vegetables, fruit, nuts, seeds, lentils, pulses, eggs, and dairy products provide a wide range of nutrients that can boost the immune system and improve general health. Numerous research studies show that those who choose to go vegetarian are likely to boost their health and longevity.

For instance, vegetarians experience 30 percent less heart disease, up to 40 percent less cancer and 20 percent less premature mortality. In addition, those with a healthy vegetarian diet usually have lower blood pressure and reduced occurrence of diet-related diabetes and obesity.

WHAT ARE THE PITFALLS?

As with any diet, balance is the key to good health. Like everyone else, vegetarians need to eat a range of foods. Simply replacing the meat part of a meal with a plate of vegetables or a slab of high-fat cheese will not provide all the nutrients required by the body. A vegetarian diet can provide all the nutrients you need and it often contains higher amounts of the antioxidant vitamins C, E, and beta-carotene. However, it is advisable to make sure that you also get adequate amounts of iron, zinc, and B vitamins, especially B12. Although it is only required in small amounts, vitamin B12 is essential for maintaining the nervous system. Good sources of B12 for vegetarians are cheese and eggs, and fortified foods such as yeast extract, breakfast cereals, soymilk, sunflower-seed margarine, and textured vegetable protein.

The mineral zinc is essential for a healthy immune system and skin, and can be found in dairy products, beans, lentils, nuts, seeds (particularly pepitas), whole grains, and yeast-based foods. A vegetarian diet often contains less zinc than a meat-based one, so it is important to supplement your diet with foods that provide this mineral. Iron deficiency is one of the most prevalent nutritional problems for vegetarians and nonvegetarians alike. Iron is essential for the formation of hemoglobin, the red pigment in blood. Iron from animal sources is more readily absorbed than that found in plant sources, so it is important for vegetarians to make sure that they eat adequate amounts. Good sources include beans, lentils, whole grains, eggs, leafy green vegetables, molasses, dairy products, fortified breakfast cereals, brown rice, broccoli, and dried fruit. Vitamin C aids the absorption of iron—a glass of orange juice with a meal is a simple way of boosting your daily vitamin C intake.

above left *Grains are an important source of energy in a diet.*

below *At least two portions of fruit should be eaten every day.*

right *A healthy diet includes a balance of different foods.*

The Foods We Need

A well-balanced vegetarian diet provides all the nutrients you need for good health. It is important to achieve a good balance of nutrients—protein, carbohydrate, vitamins, minerals, and some fat. Vegetarians need to be sure that they eat a variety of protein foods such as eggs, nuts, lentils, tofu, pulses, and dairy products. Combining these with starchy foods such as potatoes, whole grains, rice, or pasta on a daily basis will ensure that you achieve the desired range of nutrients.

CEREALS, GRAINS, AND POTATOES

This diverse group of foods, also known as complex carbohydrates, includes oats, wheat, corn, millet, barley, rye, and rice, along with their derivatives such as bread and pasta. Grains have been the staple food of many civilizations for thousands of years: wheat, barley, oats, and rye in Europe; corn in America, quinoa in South America, rice in the Far East, and millet in Africa. Despite the current popularity of low-carb diets, this group of foods is our main and most important source of energy. However, there are good and bad carbohydrates: the best are the unrefined types such as whole wheat bread and pasta, brown rice, and potatoes with their skins on, which provide fiber, B vitamins, and a range of minerals, as well as plenty of sustained energy. The carbohydrates you should cut back on, or indeed avoid, are the refined sugars found in cakes, cookies, and sugary breakfast cereals, which lead to rising and falling blood sugar levels.

DAIRY AND NONDAIRY ALTERNATIVES

Cheese, milk, and yogurt are what are known as "first-class" protein foods because they contain all eight essential amino acids, required for maintenance and repair in the body. Yet, bear in mind that many dairy products, particularly cheese, cream, and butter, are also high in saturated fat. Lowfat cheese (mozzarella, feta, ricotta, and reduced-fat Cheddar, etc.), yogurt, and milk are just as good, providing calcium, vitamin A, B_{12}, and D. If you choose to avoid dairy products, there are now plenty of alternatives made from soy, nuts, and oats, which are often fortified with vitamins and minerals. Eggs are also included in this group; a maximum of 3–4 is recommended a week.

left *Proteins from dairy foods such as milk or yogurt provide essential amino acids.*

above left *Potatoes in their skins are a healthy option, providing fiber.*

FRUIT AND VEGETABLES

Fruit and vegetables should form a major part of everyone's diet, because they are a good source of vitamins, minerals and fiber and are low in fat and calories. Dried fruit is a good source of fiber and iron, but contains negligible amounts of vitamin C.

Recent research has identified a number of natural plant compounds that may play a crucial role in preventing cancer, heart disease, arthritis, and diabetes, along with many other health problems. These compounds are collectively known as phytochemicals and are also found in other plant foods such as whole grains, pulses, nuts, and seeds. To benefit fully from the range of phytochemicals, you should eat at least five different types of fruit and vegetables a day. Cruciferous vegetables such as broccoli, cabbage, Brussels sprouts, Swiss chard, and cauliflower provide a beneficial combination of antioxidants, which support the immune system, protecting

it against potentially harmful free radicals in the body. Orange, red, and yellow fresh produce are rich in the antioxidant beta-carotene and vitamin C.

It is vital to buy fruit and vegetables as fresh as possible to benefit from their range of nutrients. Buy organic, seasonal, and locally grown produce, if possible, and avoid wilted and bruised specimens; not only will they taste inferior, but their nutrients will have diminished.

above *The main nutrients in fruit are to be found just below the skin. It is healthiest to eat them raw.*

right *It is easy to boost your fiber intake with high-fiber cereals for breakfast.*

HOW MUCH FIBER?

Few people get enough fiber. On average, we eat about ½ oz/12 g of fiber a day, but the recommended amount is around ⅔–¾ oz/18–20 g. Fruit, vegetables, whole grains, pulses, and nuts are our main source of insoluble and soluble fiber. The former helps to combat constipation, while the latter can help to reduce blood cholesterol and control blood sugar levels.

The following are some simple ways to boost your fiber intake:

• Base your diet on whole wheat bread, pasta, and rice with plentiful amounts of fruit and vegetables. If feasible, avoid peeling fruit and vegetables, since the skins contain valuable fiber.

• Porridge, whole grain cereals, and granola are the perfect high-fiber way to start the day.

• Dried fruit is rich in fiber: add it to stews, cereals, yogurt, pies, cakes, and puddings—either chopped or puréed.

• Add beans and lentils to soups, stews, bakes, and pies to boost their fiber content.

FIVE-A-DAY

The World Health Organization (WHO) recommends that we eat five portions of fruit and vegetables a day. Adults are advised to eat three different types of vegetables and two fruit, while for children it is the other way round, since they require the additional energy that fruit provides. Choose five portions made up of the following:

- 1 medium apple, pear, peach, banana, orange
- 2 satsumas, plums
- 12–15 cherries, grapes
- 1 slice melon, pineapple
- 2–3 tablespoons fruit salad
- 1 tablespoon dried fruit
- 2 tablespoons vegetables—fresh, frozen, canned
- ½ bell pepper
- 1 medium tomato
- ⅔ cup glass fruit/vegetable juice

PULSES

Dried peas, beans, and lentils are known as pulses and form a valuable part of a vegetarian diet, since they contain a higher proportion of protein than most other plant foods. They are also an important source of B vitamins, iron, calcium, zinc, and fiber, as well as being low in fat. Don't feel you have to spend hours soaking dried pulses; there is much to be said for canned ones: they taste good, are incredibly convenient, and dispense with lengthy cooking and soaking times. Additionally, canned pulses retain about half their

vitamin C content after processing, yet this diminishes almost completely when dried. If you choose to soak and boil your own, cook double the quantity required and freeze for later use.

The soybean is nutritionally superior to other types of pulse, since it is a complete protein (contains all eight essential amino acids) and is higher in iron and calcium. Tofu, tempeh, miso, soymilk, yogurt, and soy mince can all make invaluable, nutritious additions to a meatfree diet.

Lentils come in various types and are versatile, nutritious, and easy to cook. Try adding to soups, stews, and bakes to boost their protein content.

NUTS AND SEEDS

A good source of B vitamins, iron, magnesium, calcium, vitamin E, selenium, potassium, zinc, and omega-6 essential fatty acids, nuts and seeds also provide valuable protein. Peanuts and coconuts, though, are high in saturated fat, so eat in moderation. Opt for unsalted nuts; not only do they make a nutritious snack, but also give a healthy boost to pies, stews, desserts,

left *Pulses are a valuable and versatile source of protein in a vegetarian diet.*

below *Red lentils, being split, are quicker to cook from dried than other types.*

and cakes. In Chinese medicine, walnuts are known as the "longevity fruit" and are one of the few plant foods that provide both omega-3 and omega-6 essential fatty acids (EFAs). Pepitas also include both types of EFAs, while Brazil nuts and sunflower and sesame seeds, and their oils, are particularly rich in omega-6 fatty acids. Buy them as fresh as possible, preferably in their shells, since they can become rancid if stored for too long, and keep in an airtight container, away from the light.

WARNING
Nuts can be the cause of a severe allergy with life-threatening symptoms. If there is any history of nut allergy within your family, consult your doctor before giving nuts to your child. Children under five should not be given whole nuts due to the risk of choking.

above *Although high in saturated fats, nuts contain plenty of nutrients.*

left *Fats and oils are essential for the body in moderate amounts.*

FATS AND OILS
We all know that too much fat is bad for us, but a moderate amount of the appropriate type is essential for a healthy brain and eyes, keeping tissues in good repair, for the production of hormones, and to transport some vitamins around the body. A high intake of saturated fat is linked to raised cholesterol levels and heart disease, whereas unsaturated (mono- and polyunsaturated) fat can help to reduce harmful cholesterol levels in the body. Polyunsaturated fats provide the much talked about essential fatty acids omega-3 and omega-6. Fish oils are the richest source of omega-3 fatty acids. Although omega-3 is not so widely available in a vegetarian diet, you need not miss out: linseeds and flax seed oil, rapeseed oil, walnuts, eggs, pepitas, and tofu provide varying amounts. It may also be worth considering taking a suitable supplement. Omega-6 is provided by plant oils, nuts, and seeds, while olive oil is a monounsaturated fat.

WHAT YOU SHOULD EAT EVERY DAY...

- 5 or more servings of fruit and vegetables
- 3–4 servings of cereals/grains or potatoes
- 2–3 servings of pulses, nuts, and seeds
- 2 servings of milk, cheese, eggs, or soy products
- A small amount of fat/oils, such as olive, sunflower-seed, butter, or unhydrogenated margarine

Source: The Vegetarian Society

Essential Vitamins and Minerals

VITAMIN/MINERAL	FUNCTION	GOOD VEGETARIAN SOURCES	PROBLEMS CAUSED BY DEFICIENCY
VITAMIN A (retinol in animal foods, beta-carotene in plant foods)	For healthy vision, bone growth, skin, and tissue repair. Beta-carotene acts as an antioxidant and supports the immune system	Dairy products, egg yolk, margarine, carrots, apricots, squash, red bell peppers, broccoli, green leafy vegetables, mango, dried apricots, and sweet potatoes	Poor night vision, dry skin, and impaired immune system, especially respiratory disorders
VITAMIN B1 (thiamine)	Essential for breaking down carbohydrates for energy as well as the nervous system, muscles, and heart, promotes growth, and boosts mental well-being	Whole grain cereals, brewer's yeast, yeast extract, Brazil nuts, sunflower seeds, peanuts, rice, bran, and mycoprotein (Quorn®)	Depression, irritability, nervous disorders, memory loss. Common among alcoholics
VITAMIN B2 (riboflavin)	Essential for energy production as well as healthy skin, tissue repair, and maintenance	Cheese, eggs, milk, yogurt, fortified breakfast cereals, yeast extract, almonds, whole wheat bread, mushrooms, prunes, cashews, and pepitas	Lack of energy, skin problems, dry cracked lips, numbness, and itchy eyes
VITAMIN B3 (niacin)	Essential for energy production, healthy digestive system, skin, and nervous system	Pulses, yeast extract, potatoes, fortified breakfast cereals, wheat germ, peanuts, cheese, eggs, mushrooms, green leafy vegetables, figs, prunes, and sesame seeds	Deficiency is unusual, but characterized by lack of energy, depression and scaly skin
VITAMIN B6 (pyridoxine)	Essential for assimilating protein and fat, red blood cell formation, and a healthy immune system	Eggs, wheat germ, whole wheat flour, yeast extract, breakfast cereals, peanuts, bananas, currants, and lentils	Anemia, dermatitis, and depression
VITAMIN B12 (cyanocobalamin)	Essential for red blood cell formation, growth, healthy nervous system, and energy formation	Dairy products, eggs, fortified breakfast cereals, cheese, yeast extract, fortified soymilk	Fatigue, poor resistance to infection, breathlessness, and anemia
Folate (folic acid)	Essential for red blood cell formation, making genetic material (DNA), and protein synthesis. Extra is needed preconception and during pregnancy to protect fetus against neural tube defects	Green leafy vegetables, broccoli, fortified breakfast cereals, bread, nuts, pulses, bananas, yeast extract, and asparagus	Anemia, appetite loss, and linked to neural defects in babies
VITAMIN C (ascorbic acid)	Essential for healthy skin, teeth, bones, gums, immune system, resistance to infection, energy production, and growth	Citrus fruit, melons, strawberries, tomatoes, broccoli, potatoes, bell peppers, and green leafy vegetables	Impaired immune system, fatigue, insomnia, and depression
VITAMIN D	Essential for healthy teeth and bones, aids absorption of calcium, and phosphate	Sunlight, nonhydrogenated vegetable margarine, vegetable oils, eggs, and dairy products	Bone and muscle weakness. Long-term shortage results in rickets

VITAMIN/MINERAL	FUNCTION	GOOD VEGETARIAN SOURCES	PROBLEMS CAUSED BY DEFICIENCY
VITAMIN E (tocopherol)	Essential for healthy skin, circulation, and maintaining cells. As an antioxidant, it protects vitamins A and C in the body	Seeds, wheat germ, nuts, vegetable oils, eggs, whole wheat bread, green leafy vegetables, oats, sunflower-seed oil, avocado, and fortified breakfast cereals	Increased risk of heart disease, strokes, and certain cancers
VITAMIN K	Essential for effective blood clotting	Spinach, cabbage, and cauliflower	Deficiency is rare
Calcium	Essential for building and maintaining bones and teeth, muscle function, and the nervous system	Dairy products, green leafy vegetables, sesame seeds, broccoli, dried fruit, pulses, almonds, spinach, watercress, and tofu	Soft and brittle bones, osteoporosis, fractures, and muscle weakness
Iron	Essential component of hemoglobin, which transports oxygen in the blood	Egg yolk, fortified breakfast cereals, green leafy vegetables, dried fruit, cashews, pulses, whole grains, tofu, pepitas, molasses, and brown rice	Anemia, fatigue, and low resistance to infection
Magnesium	Essential for healthy muscles, bones, and teeth, normal growth, and energy production	Nuts, seeds, whole grains, pulses, tofu, dried figs, dried apricots, and green vegetables	Deficiency rare, but characterized by lethargy, weak bones and muscles, depression, and irritability
Phosphorus	Essential for healthy bones and teeth, muscle function, energy production, and the assimilation of nutrients, particularly calcium	Found in most foods: milk, cheese, yogurt, eggs, nuts, seeds, pulses, and whole grains	Deficiency is rare
Potassium	Important in maintaining the body's water balance, normal blood pressure, and nerve transmission	Bananas, milk, pulses, nuts, seeds, whole grains, potatoes, fruit, and root vegetables	Weakness, thirst, fatigue, mental confusion, and raised blood pressure
Selenium	Essential for protecting against free radical damage and for red blood cell function as well as healthy hair and skin	Avocado, lentils, milk, cheese, whole wheat bread, cashews, walnuts, seaweed, and sunflower seeds	Reduced immunity
Zinc	Essential for a healthy immune system, tissue formation, normal growth, wound healing, and reproduction	Peanuts, cheese, whole grains, sunflower seeds and pepitas, pulses, milk, hard cheese, yogurt, wheat germ, and mycoprotein (Quorn®)	Impaired growth and development, slow wound healing, and loss of taste and smell

Planning Meals

The key to a good diet is variety. A balanced meal combines sufficient amounts of protein, carbohydrate, fiber, the right types of fat, vitamins, and minerals. The ideal diet includes enough calories to provide the body with vital energy, but not an excess, which leads to weight gain.

above *Stir-frying is a quick and nutritious way to cook.*

VEGETARIAN CHILDREN

There is no reason why children should not thrive on a vegetarian diet—as long as it is not based on cheese sandwiches, baked beans, and french fries. However, they do have slightly different dietary requirements from adults. Young children can find fiber difficult to digest in large amounts; too much can make a child feel full before they have been able to ingest enough nutrients and can lead to stomach upset. Fiber can also interfere with the absorption of iron, zinc, and calcium. Refined bran should not be added to a young child's diet.

Reduced-fat foods, such as skim milk and lowfat cheese, lack the much-needed calories and therefore energy required by young growing children: reduced-fat dairy products are suitable for children over two years, but younger children require the whole equivalent.

Parents are advised to give their children at least five portions of fruit and vegetables a day, but unlike adults, this should be divided as three portions of fruit and two of vegetables—fruit provides plenty of energy.

Babies and young children do not have the capacity to eat large amounts and so need to eat three small nutritious meals a day, plus two healthy snacks.

KEEPING A MEAL BALANCED

Make sure each meal contains a protein (eggs, pulses, tofu, dairy products, nuts, and seeds) and a carbohydrate (pasta, rice, whole grains, bread) element. Despite the current popularity of low-carb diets, it is recommended that at least 50 percent of a meal is carbohydrate based. Remember that many foods, such as pulses and whole grains, are a combination of protein and carbohydrate. A moderate amount of fat in the diet is essential, not only for health, but also as it contributes to the taste, texture, and palatability of food. Restrict fat levels to no more than 30 percent of your daily diet and stick to polyunsaturated fats.

Try to include at least two different types of cooked vegetables (steamed, stir-fried, microwaved, or roasted, rather than boiled) in the main meal. Or, prepare a large salad that combines a range of different types of different-colored vegetables such as arugula, watercress, spinach, beet, avocado, tomatoes, and carrot. Fruit or fruit-based desserts make a perfect, convenient end to a meal or lowfat snack.

Try not to stick to the same meals every week. Experiment with different foods and try out new recipes. Before you do your weekly grocery shop, either write down or mentally prepare a week's repertoire of meals. In this way, you can ensure that you eat a range of different foods and that you will have the correct ingredients rather than a collection of foods that do not work together.

It is a common misconception that vegetarians have to meticulously combine protein foods in every meal to achieve the correct balance of amino acids. The latest expert advice states that, provided you eat a varied range of vegetarian protein foods on a daily basis, this is sufficient; intentionally combining proteins is unnecessary.

WATCH OUT FOR...

It is always wise to check food and drink labels when grocery shopping. The following checklist is a useful reference guide.

ADDITIVES

These include emulsifiers, colorings, and flavorings, and may or may not be vegetarian. Two of the most common are E441 (gelatin), a gelling agent derived from animal parts and bones, and E120 (cochineal), made from crushed insects.

ALBUMEN

Albumen may be derived from factory-farmed eggs.

ALCOHOL

Alcohol is clarified using animal ingredients. All cask-conditioned "real" ales, some bottled, canned, and keg bitters, milds, and stouts are fined (clarified) with isinglass derived from the swim bladders of certain tropical fish. Wine may also be fined with isinglass, dried blood, egg albumen derived from factory hens, gelatin, and chitin from crab and shrimp shells. Vegetarian alternatives include bentonite, kieselguhr, kaolin, and silica gel. Nonvintage port is fined with gelatin.

ANIMAL FATS

Animal fats are sometimes found in cookies, cakes, pie dough, stock, fries, margarine, ready-meals, margarine, and ice cream. Edible fats can mean animal fats.

ASPIC

Aspic is a savory jelly derived from meat or fish.

CANDIES

Candies may contain gelatin, cochineal, and animal fats.

CHEESE

Many cheeses are produced using animal rennet, an enzyme taken from the stomach of a calf. Vegetarian cheese is made using microbial or fungal enzymes. Nonvegetarian cheese is often used in pesto, sauces, and ready-meals.

EGGS

Eggs are animal products. Some foods, such as mayonnaise or pasta, may contain factory-farmed eggs. If possible, try to buy organic, free-range eggs.

GRAVY

Gravy is made from meat juices, although vegetarian gravy mixes do exist.

JELLO

Jello usually contains animal-derived gelatin, but it is possible to buy vegetarian alternatives set with agar agar or guar gum.

MARGARINE

Margarine may contain animal-derived vitamin D3, fats, gelatin, and E numbers as well as whey.

SOFT DRINKS

Soft drinks, particularly canned orange drinks, may contain gelatin, which is used as a carrier for added beta-carotene.

SOUP

Soup may contain animal stock or fat.

SUET

Suet is animal fat, but vegetarian versions do exist.

WORCESTERSHIRE SAUCE

Most brands contain anchovies, but vegetarian versions do exist.

YOGURT, CREME FRAICHE, FROMAGE BLANC, AND ICE CREAM

Some lowfat varieties may contain gelatin.

Source: The Vegetarian Society

below *Vegetarian cheeses are readily available in stores and supermarkets.*

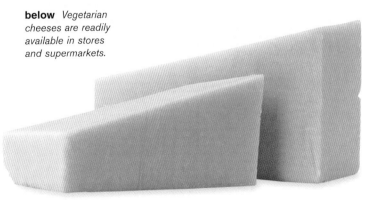

The Vegetarian Kitchen

If you have a well-stocked pantry, refrigerator, and freezer, then creating healthy, nutritious vegetarian meals is very much easier. What is equally essential is buying good-quality ingredients, then storing, preparing, and cooking them in a way that preserves as many nutrients as possible.

THE PANTRY

This list of ingredients creates a well-stocked pantry. It is by no means exhaustive, or you may feel that not all the foods are to your liking, but it gives a general guide to the foods to choose from.
• Canned pulses and vegetables: cannellini, flageolet, chickpeas, cranberry, kidney, lima beans, lentils, tomatoes, corn, ratatouille, artichokes, olives, and asparagus.
• Jars of sauces: black bean sauce, teriyaki sauce, hoisin, pesto, strained canned tomatoes, and satay sauce.
• Jars and tubes of flavorings: harissa (chili paste), tomato paste, sun-dried tomato paste, soy sauce, tamari, vegetarian Worcestershire sauce, olive paste, sweet chili sauce, miso, mustards, and mayonnaise.
• Stock-based flavorings: vegetable bouillon, miso sachets, cubes.
• Flours: all-purpose, self-rising whole wheat, white, buckwheat, glutenfree, cornmeal, and cornstarch.
• Dried pulses and lentils: chickpeas, kidney, azuki, cannellini, etc., textured vegetable protein, soy chunks or mince, as well as Puy, red, and yellow lentils.
• Dried fruit: apricots, figs, prunes, dates, apples, and raisins.
• Nuts and seeds: nut butters, walnuts, Brazils, cashews, chopped mixed nuts, ground and sliced almonds, sunflower, pepitas, and sesame seeds.
• Grains: pasta in various shapes, rice in various types, buckwheat and egg noodles, couscous, bulgur wheat, quinoa, brown, risotto, Spanish paella, basmati and pudding rice, barley, millet, and cornmeal.
• Oils and vinegars: olive (extra virgin and virgin), sunflower-seed, nut, vegetable, and sesame oils, white and red wine vinegar and cider, balsamic, and sherry wine vinegars.

above left *Pasta, rice, and cereals form an essential part of any pantry.*

above *Dried fruit keeps best if the package is well sealed.*

left *Oils and vinegars are best stored in a cool, dark place to prevent oxidation.*

- Dried herbs and spices: oregano, mixed, thyme, tarragon, saffron, coriander, cumin, chili, cardamom, cinnamon, nutmeg, cayenne, paprika, and ginger.
- Preserves and sweeteners: maple syrup, molasses, honey, fructose (natural sugar), raw brown, unrefined superfine, and confectioners' sugar, high-fruit jellies, curds, and marmalade.
- Baked goods: whole wheat crackers, oatcakes, rice cakes, corncakes, and grissini.

SHOPPING TIPS

Buy fresh foods from grocery stores with a high turnover of goods, since fruit and vegetables that have been hanging around for a while are likely to be lower in vitamins and minerals. Avoid fruit and vegetables displayed in a hot, light window, since this will influence nutrient levels. Loose fresh produce is much easier to check for quality.

When buying eggs, look for organic and free-range; not only are the hens kept in preferable living conditions, they are also fed a natural diet and are not routinely fed antibiotics or yolk-enhancing dyes.

When buying packaged foods, check the labels. Avoid those with high amounts of sugar, salt, saturated and hydrogenated (trans) fat, colorings, additives, flavorings, preservatives, and artificial sweeteners, many of which have been linked to food allergies, are unhealthy and are often not vegetarian.

Keep dry ingredients, including beans, grains, nuts, and seeds, in small quantities and store in airtight containers in a cool, dark cupboard. If kept for too long, they can become rancid. Buy oils preferably in dark bottles and store in a cool, dark place to prevent oxidation.

GET COOKING

The way you cook and prepare food influences its nutritional content. Generally speaking, raw fruit and vegetables are richer in nutrients than cooked, but avoid peeling them, if possible, since many nutrients are found in or just below the skin. Wash or scrub vegetables, but do not soak them, as water-soluble nutrients will leach into the water. When preparing fruit and vegetables, do so just before cooking or serving, as nutrients such as vitamin C diminish as soon as the cut surface is exposed to air. Steam or stir-fry foods rather than boil them—the latter destroys water-soluble vitamins such as B and C. The cooking water can also be used as stock for soup or sauces.

above left *Keeping a supply of nutritious crackers is a good idea.*

above *Buying loose produce keeps a check on the quality.*

GO ORGANIC

You may have to pay slightly more for organic produce, but the benefits are numerous. Organic fruit and vegetables tend to taste better because they are not intensively grown to absorb excessive water. They are generally cultivated in better-quality soil and left to ripen longer on the plant, rather than being artificially ripened, which can affect flavor and nutrient levels. Furthermore, some studies have shown that the lower levels of water in organic produce mean there is a higher concentration of vitamins and minerals. Children are believed to be more vulnerable to the effects of pesticide residues than adults.

Vegetables

Vegetables are an essential component of a healthy diet and have numerous nutritional benefits. It is recommended that we eat three different types of vegetable a day and there is no shortage of varieties to choose from. Vegetables offer the vegetarian cook an infinite number of culinary possibilities.

BRASSICAS

This large and varied group of vegetables boasts an extraordinary range of health properties and should form a regular part of our diet—at least 3–4 times a week. They provide numerous phytochemicals, a group of compounds that have been found to provide an anticarcinogenic cocktail and play a crucial role in fighting disease by stimulating the body's defences. Brassicas are best cooked lightly. Overcooking them not only destroys many of the nutrients, but also affects their flavor. Steaming or stir-frying are preferable to boiling for this reason. Some people dislike brassicas due to their slight bitterness, but serving them in a cream or cheese sauce may help. They also work well in Asian dishes.

CABBAGE

When lightly cooked or served shredded in a salad, cabbage is delicious. Cabbages range from the crinkly leaved Savoy, which is ideal for stuffing, to the smooth and firm white and red. Add a little vinegar to the cooking water when preparing red cabbage to preserve its color. Chinese cabbage has a more delicate flavor and is good in salads or stir-fries.

BROCCOLI

There are two types of broccoli: the slender-stemmed purple sprouting type and the readily available calabrese, with its tightly budded top and thick stalk. Choose broccoli with dark green or purple florets and avoid any with signs of yellowing or a wilted stalk. When serving broccoli, do not forget the stalk, which is also nutritious. The stalk can be served raw; grated into salads or cut into crudités.

CAULIFLOWER

Cauliflower comes in many varieties, ranging from white to pale green and purple, but all should be encased in green outer leaves, as these protect the more delicate florets.

BRUSSELS SPROUTS

Reminiscent of Christmas, Brussels sprouts are like miniature cabbages and have a strong, nutty flavor. Sprouts are sweeter when picked after the first frost. They are best cooked very lightly or, better still, stir-fried.

LEAFY GREENS

Research into the health benefits of leafy greens shows that by eating spinach, Swiss chard, bok choy, spring greens, and spinach beet on a regular basis, you may protect yourself against certain forms of cancer. Leafy vegetables are tastiest served steamed or stir-fried and go particularly well with Asian dishes that include garlic, ginger, chili, and soy sauce.

SHOOT VEGETABLES

This diverse group includes asparagus, fennel, chicory, celery, and the globe artichoke. The distinguished globe artichoke has an exquisite flavor and is great fun to eat: simply boil in water, then dip each leaf into garlic butter or mayonnaise, or a vinaigrette dressing. The tastiest part is the heart, which is to be found in the center of the vegetable, beneath the hairy choke.

SPINACH

Spinach does provide iron, but not in such rich amounts as was once thought and in a form that is not easy to assimilate. However, combining spinach with vitamin C-rich foods increases absorption. Nutritionally, spinach is most beneficial when eaten raw and the young leaves are best for this.

SWISS CHARD

Like spinach, Swiss chard should have dark green leaves and a white or red stem. As the stem takes longer to cook than the leaves, it is best sliced and cooked slightly before the leaves. Spinach beet is similar to Swiss chard and has a mild flavor. Spring greens are full of flavor and nutrients and should have dark green leaves.

BOK CHOY

The most typical bok choy features dark green leaves at the top of thick, white, upright stalks. It has a mild flavor, which makes it popular with children, and makes a delightful addition to stir-fries, soups, noodle dishes, and salads. The stalk takes slightly longer to cook than the leaves.

ASPARAGUS

There are two types of asparagus: white is picked just before the sprouts reach the surface of the soil, while green-tipped is cut above the ground and develops its color when it comes into contact with sunlight. Before briefly steaming, boiling, griddling, or roasting, trim off the woody end.

CELERY

Celery lends a crunchy texture to salads and also makes a good base for soups and stews. Green celery is available all year round, and white is available in winter. Choose stems that are very firm and rigid, but don't forget the leaves, which have a tangy flavor and can be added to stocks. Celery hearts can also be braised.

CHICORY

The long, tightly packed leaves of red or white chicory have a distinctive, bitter taste so use sparingly. Trim the root, remove the core and slice thinly. Chicory can be served raw in salads, steamed or braised.

FENNEL

Fennel has a mild anise flavor, which is most potent when eaten raw. Roasting fennel (cut into wedges) tempers the flavor and adds a delicious sweetness. It also goes well with Mediterranean flavors such as tomatoes, olive oil, garlic, and basil.

MUSHROOMS

There is a wide range of mushrooms to choose from, both fresh and dried, and even many types of wild mushroom are now cultivated. The most popular are the mild-flavored button-capped, and the field mushroom, which has a more earthy, intense flavor. Buy mushrooms that are firm and smell fresh; avoid ones that have slimy, damp patches. Dried mushrooms keep well: to reconstitute them, soak in boiling water for 20–30 minutes. Drain and rinse well to remove any dirt and grit. Use the soaking water in stocks and sauces, but strain first.

CEPES

Cèpes (or porcini) have a meaty texture and woody flavor. Dried cèpes lend a rich flavor to soups, stocks, and sauces.

CHANTERELLE

Golden-colored chanterelle (or girolle) mushrooms have a delicate flavor. They should be wiped rather than washed, as they are very porous. Most types of mushroom should be prepared in this way, apart from the honeycomb-capped morel.

SHIITAKE AND OYSTER

Both shiitake and oyster mushrooms are now widely cultivated. Oyster are fluted in shape, and while they are

usually grayish-brown in color, they also come in pale yellow and pink. Shiitake have a chewy texture and robust flavor, and are most commonly used in Asian dishes.

HOW TO PREPARE FRESH MUSHROOMS

It is best not to wash mushrooms, or you risk making them soggy and unappetizing. Instead, trim off the stalks, then wipe the caps with a piece of moistened paper towel to remove any soil or compost. Some mushrooms are grown in a sandy medium, which is difficult to remove by wiping. Plunge the mushrooms into a bowl of cold water and any sand will sink. Shake well before drying with paper towels.

ROOT VEGETABLES

The comfort foods of the vegetable world, potatoes, carrots, rutabaga, celery root, beet, and parsnips, among others, have a sweet, dense flesh that provides a range of vitamins and minerals, not forgetting fiber.

POTATOES

There are hundreds of different potato varieties and many lend themselves to particular cooking methods. Waxy potatoes, like Round Reds, are best boiled, or try roasting them whole, while mealy varieties, like Russets, lend themselves to roasting, baking, and mashing. Stored in a dark, well-ventilated place, potatoes will keep for about two weeks. Sweet potatoes have an orange or white flesh (the former is richer in beta-carotene). When cooked, the white-fleshed variety has a drier texture, but both are good roasted, mashed, or baked.

LETTUCES
Romaine and iceberg have firm, crisp leaves, while Boston is a smaller, sweeter version of romaine. The pretty frilly leaves of lollo rosso are green at the base and a deep red around the edge. Equally attractive is the oak leaf. Nutritionally, lettuce is best eaten raw, with the darker outer leaves containing more nutrients than the pale-colored inner. However, it can also be braised, steamed, and turned into soups.

OTHER SALAD GREENS
Cress, mizuna, arugula, and watercress have a strong, distinctive flavor and will enliven any salad. Escarole, frisée, and radicchio are slightly bitter in flavor and are best used in moderation as they can easily dominate a salad.

FRUIT VEGETABLES
Tomatoes, eggplants, chilies, avocados, and bell peppers are all vegetables, but botanically they are classified as fruit. This group adds plenty of color and flavor to a range of dishes. Known in the Middle East as "poor man's caviar," eggplants give substance and flavor to stews and tomato-based bakes, and can be roasted, broiled, or puréed into garlicky dips.

TOMATOES
There are now so many varieties of tomato to choose, from the sweet, bite-size cherry to the large beefsteak. The egg-shaped plum tomato makes rich sauces, while sun-dried tomatoes add a richness to dips, sauces, soups, and stews.

CARROTS AND BEET
When buying carrots and beet, remember that the smaller ones are sweeter. Raw carrots and beet can be grated into salads or used to make relishes. Roasting them intensifies their sweetness and both work well in soups.

CELERY ROOT
Celery root is a knobbly root with a flavor reminiscent of celery. Peel and grate raw into salads, steam, bake, or combine with potatoes to make a delicious mash.

JERUSALEM ARTICHOKES
These small, knobbly tubers have a mild, nutty flavor and are delicious roasted or transformed into soup. Scrub rather than peel before use.

SALAD GREENS
Salad greens come in a huge variety of shapes, textures, colors, and flavors, from the bitter-tasting endive to peppery watercress and delicate butterhead lettuce. Convenient bags of mixed salad greens allow you to sample a wide range of different types, although they do not tend to last as long as the individually packed types.

CHILIES

Chilies form a crucial role in many cuisines, including Mexican, Indian, and Thai. There are hundreds of different types, which range in potency from the mild and flavorful to the blisteringly hot.

BELL PEPPERS

Red, yellow, and orange bell peppers are an excellent source of vitamin C, the green and purple to a lesser extent. Green bell peppers are fully developed, but are not as ripe as their more colorful counterparts, which can make them relatively difficult to digest.

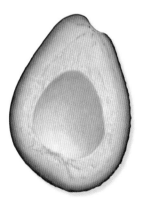

AVOCADOS

Avocados are rich in vitamins C and E and are said to improve the condition of the skin and hair. Brush with lemon or lime juice after cutting to prevent the flesh turning brown. They are usually served raw, but can also be baked.

PODS AND SEEDS

The vegetables in this category, such as peas, green beans, snow peas, sugar snap peas, fava beans, and corn, all have a good nutritional value.

PEAS

Peas are one of the few vegetables that taste as good when cooked from frozen as when cooked fresh.

FAVA BEANS

Fava beans are best when very fresh and young. Tiny pods can be eaten whole, while when slightly older, you may prefer to pop the bean out of its tough shell after cooking to reveal a succulent green bean.

STRING BEANS

When buying green beans (string, green, and dwarf), look for good color and avoid any signs of discoloration or wilting. Simply trim, then steam until just tender. They are delicious when served as a warm salad with a dressing made of ginger, garlic, sesame oil, and rice wine vinegar.

CORN

These are best eaten soon after picking and after purchase, before the natural sugars have started to convert into starch and lose their sweetness, and the kernels toughen. Preferably buy corncobs still encased in their green husks, which help to keep them fresh.

ONION FAMILY

Onions, garlic, leeks, shallots, and scallions add plenty of flavor to all manner of savory vegetarian dishes and can also be cooked on their own. Onions and garlic should be stored in a cool, dry, airy place away from direct sunlight.

ONIONS

These provide potent antioxidants and are said to reduce health-threatening cholesterol levels in the body. Cooking tempers the pungency of the onion family, while roasting brings out their delicious sweetness. Onions offer a range of taste sensations from the sweet and mild Spanish white onion and light and fresh scallion to the versatile and pungent yellow onion. Pearl onions and shallots are the smallest.

PUMPKIN AND SQUASH

This group of vegetables comes in a wide range of colors, shapes, and sizes. They are broadly divided into two types: summer, which include cucumbers, zucchini, and marrows; and winter, such as the various pumpkins and squashes.

HOW TO PREPARE PUMPKIN AND SQUASH

These vegetables have thick skins, which are usually removed before cooking. Select a large, heavy knife and put a damp dish towel under the cutting board so that it doesn't slip. Cut off a slice from the bottom, to give you a flat base, and cut off the stalk end, too. Stand the vegetable on the base and cut away the tough skin with firm, vertical slices for butternut squash or following the curve for round varieties and pumpkins. Then slice in half and use a large spoon to scrape out all the seeds and fibers. Dice or slice the flesh.

SUMMER

Zucchini are at their best when small and young; the flavor diminishes the older and larger they get and the seeds toughen. Extremely versatile, zucchini can be steamed, stir-fried, puréed, griddled, and roasted, as well as used in soups and casseroles. Their deep yellow flowers are perfect for stuffing. Look for firm, bright, unblemished vegetables that are heavy for their size.

WINTER

Butternut squash is one of the most readily available winter types. A large, distinctively pear-shaped vegetable with a golden skin and orange flesh, it is equally delicious mashed, baked, or roasted, or used in soups and stews, and makes a good substitute for pumpkin. Small pumpkins have a sweeter, less fibrous flesh than the large ones, which are probably best kept for making lanterns at Halloween!

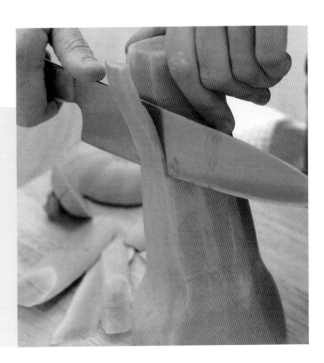

Fruit

The range of fruit we have to choose from is incredibly diverse. It is easy to buy the same types every week, but it really is worth experimenting with new varieties. The ultimate convenience food, most fruit simply needs a wash and is ready to eat. As most nutrients are found just below the skin, avoid peeling if possible and preferably eat raw rather than cooked, as the latter affects nutrient levels. Good quality and freshness is essential when buying fruit; not only will it taste better and last longer, but it will be higher in antioxidant nutrients. Buy organic whenever you can and avoid bulk-buying if the fruit is going to sit in the fruit bowl or refrigerator for days.

CITRUS FRUIT

Vibrantly colored oranges, lemons, grapefruit, clementines, and limes are packed with beneficial vitamin C and beta-carotene. They make a versatile addition to the kitchen, lending themselves to both sweet and savory dishes. Once cut or peeled, use straight away, as vitamin C levels diminish from the moment they are sliced into.

ORANGES

Popular varieties of orange include the juicy Jaffa, Valencia, and navel (named after the belly button-type spot at the flower end). Thin-skinned oranges tend to be the juiciest. Marmalade is made from the sour-tasting Seville orange. Orange rind or peel adds a fragrant note to cakes, cookies, and sweet sauces, as well as savory dishes.

LEMONS

Lemons (juice and rind) are an essential ingredient in the kitchen; just a squeeze of juice will add zing to salad dressings, vegetables, and marinades. The rind also enlivens both sweet and savory dishes. Lemon juice can also prevent some fruit and vegetables, such as avocado and apples, discoloring when cut. Avoid those with green patches on the skin, as this is a sign of unripeness.

LIMES

Limes have a sharper flavor than lemons and are often used in Indian, Indonesian, and Thai cooking, adding a fragrant note.

HOW TO SEGMENT CITRUS FRUIT

Use a serrated knife to cut off a slice from the top and bottom of the fruit to reveal the flesh.

Remove the skin and white pith, either in a spiral, beginning at the cut top and following the curve of the fruit, or by standing the fruit on the cut base and cutting down from top to bottom around the fruit.

Hold the fruit in the palm of your hand over a bowl. Use a small fruit knife to cut in front of the membrane. Push the knife forward to remove the segment cleanly from the membrane. Cut in front of the next membrane, then again push the knife forward toward the outer edge of the fruit—the segment will drop into the bowl.

Continue to separate all the segments from the membrane, then squeeze the membrane tightly. Unless using the segments immediately, put in a small bowl, cover with plastic wrap, and refrigerate to prevent the air oxidizing the fruit and making it bitter.

ORCHARD FRUIT

Probably the most popular group of fruit, ranging from crisp apples to succulent peaches and juicy cherries. There are hundreds of different varieties of apple, and while we only see a mere fraction of these, many stores are now beginning to stock more unusual types. Rome Beauty and Newtown Pippin are popular cooking apples, and may require sweetening with sugar. Some eating apples are equally good stewed in a little water and no extra sugar is required.

PEACHES

Gorgeous succulent peaches range in color from gold to deep red and the flesh can be golden or white. Nectarines are similar, but without the fuzzy skin. Buy both peaches and nectarines slightly hard and then ripen them at home. They bruise easily, so care is needed.

PEARS

Like certain apples, some varieties of pear are good for cooking, while others are best eaten raw. Pears are best in the late summer and fall with the arrival of the new season's crop. Particular favorites are the plump Comice, yellow-green-skinned Anjou, and yellow-skinned Bosc.

CHERRIES

Glossy, sweet red cherries make a welcome appearance in stores in the summer months. There are two types: sweet and sour. The latter is best cooked.

PLUMS

Plums are a popular summer fruit that vary in color and flavor from the sweet and juicy to the slightly tart. The latter are best cooked in pies and cakes.

CURRANTS

These tiny baubles of brightly colored fruit make a pretty addition to desserts. Black currants, white currants, and red currants are usually sold in bunches on the stem. To remove the currants from the stalk, run the tines of a fork down through the clusters, taking care not to damage the fruit. They can be on the tart side and may need a sprinkling of sugar. Currants look attractive in fruit salads, pies, and summer pudding, or can be transformed into jellies and jams.

BERRIES

Usually at their best in the summer, berries are mostly available all year round.

STRAWBERRIES

Strawberries, if at their peak of ripeness (avoid those with white or green tips), need little embellishment; simply a spoonful of cream or crème fraîche will suffice. Strawberries contain plenty of vitamin C, and are also a good source of B vitamins.

RASPBERRIES

Raspberries are very fragile and don't have a long shelf life. Their soft, delicate texture, and aromatic flavor are best suited to simple preparations.

GOOSEBERRIES

Gooseberries are a popular fruit in northern Europe, but are relatively rare in other parts of the world. They range from the tart green variety with the fuzzy skin, which is best suited to pies, crumbles, and jams, to the softer, sweeter, purple type. This can be mixed with cream or custard to make a fruit fool.

BLACKBERRIES

Blackberries, the largest of the wild berries, are cultivated throughout the United States from May until early fall. Juicy and plump, blackberries vary in sweetness. Often used in cooking, they are delicious in summer pudding, tarts, pies, crumbles, or puréed to make a sauce that goes with ice cream or nut roasts.

BLUEBERRIES

Ripe blueberries are plump and slightly firm, with a natural "bloom." They are delicious eaten raw, but can be made into jams and jellies and baked into pies, tarts, cakes, and muffins.

GRAPES

Grapes range in color from deep purple to pale red, and from vibrant green to almost white. Most grapes are grown for wine production; those for eating tend to be less acidic and have a thinner skin. Preferably buy organic grapes or wash well before eating. They should be plump and firm, and firmly attached to the stalk.

MELONS

When buying melons, look for those that are heavy for their size, yield to gentle pressure, and smell fragrant at the stem end—this is a sign of ripeness. There is a wide range to choose from, including the pinkish-red watermelon, yellow honeydew, and orange-fleshed cantaloupe. Watermelons are very low in calories due to their high water count and make a refreshing summer dessert. Avoid buying ready-cut fruit, as vitamin levels will have diminished.

TROPICAL FRUIT

This exotic collection of fruit ranges from the popular banana to the more unusual papaya.

BANANAS

The high starch content of bananas means that they provide plenty of energy as well as fiber, vitamins, and minerals. The soft, creamy flesh can be baked whole, frozen to make a quick ice cream, blended into smoothies, or mashed into cakes. Bananas with patches of green can be ripened at room temperature, but it is not advisable to buy entirely green fruit, as they rarely ripen properly.

PINEAPPLES

Pineapples have a sweet and juicy flesh. Choose fruit that are heavy for their size and are slightly tender when pressed, with fresh, green, spiky leaves. The fruit is ripe when you can successfully pull out a leaf, without tugging. Pineapples are particularly good for the digestive system.

MANGOES

Mangoes have a wonderfully fragrant, juicy pulp when ripe, which can be used in a wide range of both sweet and savory dishes, turned into smoothies, ice cream, purées, and sauces, and added to salsas and salads. The skin ranges in color from green to yellow, orange, or red. A mango that is entirely green is likely to be unripe, although in Asia these are often sliced into salads.

PAPAYAS

The slightly pear-shaped papaya has a speckled yellow skin when ripe, a vibrant pinkish-orange pulp, and an incredibly perfumed flavor. The numerous edible seeds taste peppery when dried. Papaya is best eaten raw, although unripe green fruit can be used in cooking.

KIWIFRUITS

Kiwifruit or Chinese gooseberry is particularly rich in vitamin C. The puréed flesh can be used to make refreshing sorbets and ice creams. Slice in half and scoop out the green flesh and tiny black seeds with a spoon for a healthy snack, or use in fruit salads.

PASSION FRUITS

Passion fruit does not look particularly inviting, with its dark, wrinkly skin, but inside there is a fragrant mixture of golden pulp and edible black seeds ready to be eaten.

Grains and Cereals

When we think of grains, rice, wheat, and oats immediately spring to mind, yet this group is surprisingly wide and each type comes in various forms, from the whole grain to flour. For most of us, grains form a major part of our diet and a nutritious one at that: high in complex carbohydrates, grains also contain protein, fiber, vitamins, and minerals, and are low in fat. Unprocessed types, such as whole wheat bread and pasta, are richer in these nutrients, since the refining process depletes much of their goodness. Inexpensive and readily available, they make a versatile addition to the pantry.

To ensure freshness, always buy grains and their related products from stores that have a regular turnover of stock. Store in airtight containers in a cool, dry, dark cupboard to prevent them becoming stale and to keep moisture out.

WHEAT
The most widely available grain crop in the Western world, wheat comes in various forms.

FLOUR
Flour is ground from the whole grain and may be whole wheat, brown or white, depending on the degree of processing. Strong flour is high in gluten, which makes it ideal for bread-making, while soft flour is lower in gluten and higher in starch, making it better for cakes and pastries. Durum wheat flour is one of the hardest wheat varieties and is used to make pasta.

OTHER FORMS
Other forms of wheat include wheat berries, bran, flakes, cracked wheat, bulgur wheat, semolina, wheat grass, and couscous. The latter, which looks like a grain, is actually a form of pasta made by steaming and drying cracked durum wheat.

RICE
Almost every culture in the world has its own culinary repertoire of rice dishes, ranging from Spanish paella to Indian biryani.

LONG-GRAIN AND BROWN RICE
Long-grain is the most widely used type of rice; brown rice has a nutty, chewier texture than white, which contains less fiber and fewer nutrients.

BASMATI
Basmati, available both brown and white, is a slender, long-grain rice and is aged for a year after harvest. Widely used in Indian dishes, its light, fluffy grain is also good for rice salads.

THAI AND JAPANESE RICE
Thai or jasmine rice has a soft, sticky texture and a mild, perfumed flavor—which explains its other name, fragrant rice. Japanese rice also has a soft, sticky texture and is mixed with rice vinegar to make sushi rolls.

ARBORIO, CARNAROLI, AND VALENCIA

Arborio and Carnaroli are classic risotto rices. The short, stubby grain absorbs about five times its weight in water, creating a creamy result. Spanish rice, used for paella, is also a short-grain rice, but it is not quite as starchy as risotto rice.

OTHER FORMS

Other forms to look out for are red rice, wild pecan rice, and wild rice; the latter, with its slender black grains, is not in fact a true rice but an aquatic grass.

STORING AND REUSING COOKED RICE

Leftover cooked rice can be kept in an airtight container in the refrigerator. Make sure it is thoroughly cooled before refrigerating. If it is being used cold in salads, chill and use within a day. Reheat cooked rice thoroughly. Microwave it until piping hot or tip the rice into a pan of boiling water and reheat it for 1 minute only, or steam it over boiling water. Cooked rice is susceptible to a bacteria, *Bacillus cereus*, which can cause stomach upsets if not used within 2 days.

OTHER GRAINS
OATS

Like rye, oats are a popular grain in Northern Europe. Flaked and rolled oats are used to make porridge and granola. Medium and fine oatmeal is best in oatcakes and breads. Oats are believed to reduce cholesterol levels in the blood.

CORN

Also known as maize, corn comes in yellow, blue, red, and black varieties. We are most familiar with yellow corn, which is used for cornmeal or polenta, cornstarch, and popcorn.

RYE

Rye flour is commonly used to make a dark, dense bread, particularly in Eastern Europe, Scandinavia, and Russia. The strong-tasting grain can also be used in savory dishes.

QUINOA

This highly nutritious grain is one of the few plant foods that is a complete protein, which means it contains all eight essential amino acids. The tiny bead-type grain has a mild, slightly bitter taste and can be used to make tabbouleh, stuffings, bakes, pilafs, and breakfast cereals.

MILLET

This grain is not widely used, but it is highly nutritious, containing more iron than most other grains. It is also a good source of zinc. The tiny beadlike grains have a mild flavor and make the perfect accompaniment to stews and curries, and can be used in pilafs, tabbouleh, milk puddings, and porridge. It is also glutenfree.

BARLEY

Pearl barley is the most common form and is husked, steamed, and polished to give it its characteristic ivory-colored look. Pot barley is the whole grain and takes much longer to cook than pearl. Both types make a satisfying porridge and can be added to stews, bakes, and soups.

Pulses and Beans

Lentils, beans, and peas are all pulses and are an excellent source of lowfat protein as well as complex carbohydrates, vitamins, minerals, and fiber. Their versatility and ability to absorb the flavors of other foods mean that they can form the base of a great number of different dishes. Although pulses can be kept for up to a year, they do tend to toughen with time. Buy from stores with a high turnover of stock and look for bright, unwrinkled pulses that are not dusty. Store pulses in an airtight container in a cool, dark place and rinse before use. Avoid adding salt to the water when cooking, as this prevents them from softening; instead, season when cooked.

LENTILS
Unlike most other pulses, lentils do not require presoaking and are relatively quick to cook. They are sold dried or canned and can be used in a variety of dishes—dals, burgers, bakes, stews, and soups.

GREEN LENTILS
Similar to the brown lentil, green lentils have a slightly milder flavor and can be cooked and blended with herbs and garlic to make a nutritious spread. The tiny, dark, gray-green Puy lentil is grown in France and is considered superior in flavor to other varieties. They take around 25–30 minutes to cook, but retain their beadlike shape. They are delicious in warm salads with a vinaigrette dressing and also make a hearty addition to stews.

DRIED PEAS
Unlike lentils, peas are soft when young and need to be dried. Available whole or split, the latter has a sweeter flavor and cooks more quickly.

SPLIT LENTILS
Orange-colored red lentils are the most familiar variety, and because they are "split," they can be cooked in around 20 minutes, eventually disintegrating into a thick purée. They are ideal for thickening soups and stews, and are used to make the spicy Indian dish, dal.

YELLOW AND GREEN SPLIT PEAS
Yellow and green split peas are interchangeable with red split lentils and are perfect for dals, soups, casseroles, and purées, but they do take slightly longer to cook.

BROWN LENTILS
These disk-shaped lentils, sometimes called Continental lentils, have a robust texture and flavor. Available whole, they take longer to cook than red lentils—around 45 minutes—and add substance to stews, stuffings, and soups.

MARROW FAT PEAS
Marrow fat peas are larger in size and are used to make the British classic "mushy" peas. They should be soaked overnight before cooking.

BEANS

With the exception of the ubiquitous baked (haricot) bean, beans are often ignored, yet they are all so versatile, lending themselves to pies, bakes, stews, soups, pâtés, dips, burgers, salads, and more. What often puts people off is the long soaking time—usually overnight—but canned beans are just as good and incredibly convenient. Just drain and rinse before use.

CHICKPEAS

Chickpeas resemble shelled hazelnuts and have a nutty flavor and a creamy texture. They are widely used in Indian and Middle Eastern cuisines. In India, they are ground to make the yellow-colored gram flour, which is used for making fritters and flat breads.

FLAGEOLET AND CRANBERRY

The pretty, pale green flageolet bean has a fresh, delicate taste and soft texture, while the hearty cranberry bean is pinkish-brown in color with a sweetish flavor and tender texture, often used to make Italian bean and pasta soups.

CANNELLINI

Cannellini beans are white, kidney-shaped beans, which have a soft, creamy texture when cooked. They are equally delicious served warm in salads or puréed to make a tasty, nutritious alternative to mash.

RED KIDNEY

Red kidney beans have a soft, "mealy" texture and retain their color and shape when cooked. They are used to make Mexican refried beans and are essential to a successful chili.

HARICOT

Haricot beans (navy or Boston beans) are most commonly eaten as canned baked beans, but the ivory-colored bean is also good in stews and soups.

LIMA

Lima beans are cream-colored, kidney-shaped beans with a soft, floury texture, and are available fresh, frozen, canned, and dried. In the South, lima beans are also called butter beans.

SOYBEANS

This versatile bean has all the nutritional properties of animal products, but none of the disadvantages. They range in color from creamy yellow through to brown-black and make a healthy addition to soups, casseroles, and bakes. The dried beans are very dense and need to be soaked for 12 hours before cooking.

Soybeans are also used to make tofu, tempeh, meat-replacement mince and chunks, flour, soymilk, soy sauce, and miso, as well as a range of sauces, including black bean sauce, yellow bean sauce, and hoisin sauce.

COOKING BEANS

Once soaked, beans should be drained and rinsed in clean water. Any pulses that have floated to the surface during soaking should be discarded. You need to allow plenty of water for cooking: 5 cups fresh cold water per 1 lb/450 g beans. Bring to a boil over high heat and boil for 10 minutes, then reduce the heat and let simmer until the beans are soft but not mushy, which can take anything from 30 minutes to 2 hours, depending on the type and age of the bean. The beans must always be submerged: top off with boiling water to keep them covered by about ½ inch/ 1 cm as necessary. The cooking water can be used as a vegetable stock. If you are cooking more than one variety of bean, they need to be soaked and cooked separately, as they will cook at different rates. Remember to add salt only toward the end of cooking.

Dairy Products

Dairy produce provides vegetarians with valuable protein as well as calcium and vitamins D and B, including B12. Many dairy products are high in fat and therefore should be eaten sparingly, or alternatively, you can opt for reduced-fat alternatives. For those who do not eat dairy products, there are an increasing number of substitutes to choose from, which have similar culinary properties.

MILK, CREAM, AND YOGURT

MILK

Cow's milk is one of our most widely used ingredients. Skim and lowfat versions now outsell their whole counterpart, yet they are not nutritionally inferior. Organic milk is now widely available, and comes from cows that have been fed a pesticidefree diet and are not routinely treated with hormones. For those who are intolerant of cow's milk, there is goat and sheep's milk, which are nutritionally similar, but easier to digest.

CREAM

The fat content of cream varies enormously, ranging from about 12 percent for half-fat through to a decadent 55 percent for clotted cream. Crème fraîche is a rich, cultured cream with a fat content of around 35 percent, yet now comes in half-fat versions (around 10 percent). A spoonful adds a delicious creaminess to sauces or dolloped onto fresh fruit, especially strawberries. Sour cream is treated with lactic acid, which gives it its characteristic tang. It contains 20 percent fat, although it is possible to buy reduced-fat versions. If using in cooking, take care that it does not curdle.

YOGURT

The fat content of yogurt ranges from 0.5 g per 100 g through to 10 g per 100 g for thick strained plain yogurt. Although the latter is higher in fat than most types of yogurt, it is lower in fat than cream and makes a useful replacement in cooking, as it does not curdle, unlike lowfat varieties. Plain yogurts have been fermented with beneficial bacteria that can aid digestion and have a mild, creamy flavor.

NONDAIRY ALTERNATIVES

It is important for vegans in particular to ensure their diet includes the protein, minerals, and vitamins found in dairy products. The best source is the soybean. Tofu, or soy cheese, made from cooked soybeans, is an excellent nonmeat protein that is cholesterolfree. As well as being a useful source of calcium, tofu also contains vitamin E, manganese, phosphorus, and iron. Milk, cream, and yogurt products are also made from dried soybeans. Other products that are nutritionally similar to cow's milk are milk and cheese substitutes made from oats, rice, and nuts. Pure vegetable margarines and spreads are also available.

FRESH UNRIPENED CHEESES

Young, immature cheeses are unlikely to contain rennet and have a light, mild flavor.

COTTAGE CHEESE

Cottage cheese is a soft, fresh-curd variety of cheese and is available in large- and small-curd varieties. Cottage cheese is one of the most popular and is lower in fat—2–5 percent—than most other cheeses.

FROMAGE BLANC

Fromage blanc is a smooth, fresh cheese with the same consistency as thick yogurt, but is less acidic. The fat content varies from almost nothing to about 8 percent. It can be used in much the same way as yogurt but is hard to find.

ITALIAN RICOTTA

The Italian ricotta can be made from sheep's or cow's milk and has a slightly granular texture. Its mild, clean flavor means that it can be used in both savory and sweet dishes.

CREAM CHEESE AND QUARK

Cream cheese has a rich, velvety consistency, while Quark is a lowfat curd cheese. Both are perfect for making cheese-cakes, dips, and spreads.

FRESH RIPENED CHEESES

BRIE AND CAMEMBERT

These fresh, soft, cow's milk cheeses come predominantly from France. When fully ripe, they have an invitingly buttery texture that "oozes" inside. Camembert tends to have a stronger flavor than Brie, which is enhanced when served at room temperature.

OTHER SOFT AND HARD CHEESES

The following gives just a taster of other soft and hard cheeses that are all readily available in vegetarian rennet versions.

MOZZARELLA

Mozzarella has a delicate, silky texture, as well as excellent melting properties, hence its use on pizzas and bakes. It is usually made from cow's milk, but the traditional cheese is made from buffalo's milk and is called mozzarella di bufala.

HALLOUMI

Halloumi has been called the vegetarian alternative to bacon. It has a firm, rubbery texture and salty flavor; cut it into slices and broil or griddle. Provolone cheese is a good alternative.

FETA

Feta can be soaked in water for 10 minutes to remove its saltiness. It has a firm, crumbly texture and is used in the classic Greek salad. It was once made with goat or sheep's milk, but is now more often made with cow's milk.

CHEDDAR

Cheddar is a British favorite, but it varies tremendously in quality. Look for a good-quality sharp Cheddar, which is aged between nine and 24 months and has a rich, nutty flavor. Colby, a Wisconsin cheese, is a good alternative.

Nuts and Seeds

Nuts and seeds are more than just a convenient snack, making a useful and healthy addition to both sweet and savory vegetarian dishes. Best bought in small quantities from stores with a high turnover of goods, nuts and seeds can become rancid—especially shelled ones. Stored in an airtight container in a cool, dark place, nuts and seeds should last about three months.

NUTS

Nuts are the fruits of trees, with the exception of peanuts, which grow underground. Nuts contain essential linoleic acid (omega-6), and a range of other nutrients, including protein, B vitamins, iron, selenium, vitamin E, and zinc. Nuts are available whole, with or without shells, blanched, slivered, chopped, ground, or toasted.

BRAZIL NUTS
Brazil nuts have a sweet, milky taste and are particularly rich in omega-6 essential fatty acids. They are often used in granola-type breakfast cereals or in desserts.

MACADAMIA NUTS
Macadamia nuts have a creamy, rich, buttery flavor and a surprisingly high-fat content. The round nut is usually sold shelled, as the outer casing is extremely hard to crack.

ALMONDS
Almonds come in two types: bitter and sweet. The former is not recommended raw, but is transformed into a fragrant oil and essence. Sweet almonds are best bought shelled in their skins. You can blanch them yourself in boiling water for a few minutes to remove the skin. However, you can also buy them ready-blanched as well as slivered, toasted, and ground, all of which add a richness and pronounced flavor to cakes, desserts, and some savory dishes.

CASHEWS
Cashews are always sold without their tough outer shell and are lower in fat than most other nuts. Their creamy flavor lends itself to roasts, bakes, and nut butters, or they add a pleasant crunch when in noodle dishes and salads.

HAZELNUTS
The versatile hazelnut is sold whole, shelled, chopped, and ground, and is especially good roasted. Use in both savory and sweet dishes.

CHESTNUTS
Cooked or roasted chestnuts have a delicious sweet taste and floury texture. They add substance to stuffings, roasts, bakes, and pies. Sweetened chestnut purée is used in desserts.

PINE NUTS
One of the key ingredients in pesto is the tiny, cream-colored nut, which has a rich, creamy flavor, enhanced by toasting. Buy in small quantities as their high-fat content means that they readily become rancid.

WALNUTS

When picked young, walnuts are referred to as "wet" and have a fresh, milky kernel. However, they are usually bought dried—shelled, chopped, or ground—when the nut adopts a slightly bitter flavor.

COCONUT

Coconut is high in saturated fat, so is best eaten in moderation. Coconut milk and cream add a rich creaminess to sauces, curries, smoothies, desserts, and soups. The dense white "meat" is also made into shredded or flaked coconut.

SEEDS

Albeit tiny, seeds pack a powerful punch when it comes to their nutritional status. They are a good source of the antioxidant vitamin E and iron, as well as the essential fatty acid omega-6, which may help in reducing harmful cholesterol levels—and all that from a small and unassuming seed!

SESAME SEEDS

Tiny sesame seeds come in black or white and are used to make a surprising range of products. Ground into a thick paste, they make sesame seed paste; the base of hummus; the sweet confection halva; or are turned into a rich, toasted oil. Their flavor is improved by toasting in a dry skillet until golden. Sprinkle over salads, bakes, cakes, and breads.

SUNFLOWER SEEDS

Toasting also improves the flavor of sunflower seeds, but take care not to burn them, as their nutritional content will be affected. The tear-shaped seeds have similar uses to sesame seeds and make a healthy addition to salads, breakfast cereals, and oat cookies.

PEPITAS (PUMPKIN SEEDS)

Pepitas (pumpkin seeds) are one of the few plant foods to contain both omega-3 and omega-6 essential fatty acids and are richer in iron than other seeds. They make a nutritious snack or can be used in much the same way as other seeds.

POPPY SEEDS

The small, black poppy seed adds an attractive decorative look as well as crunch to breads and cakes. They are used in German and Eastern European pastries, strudels, and tarts.

FLAX SEEDS

Long known for its oil, used to polish wood, these small, golden seeds are also known as linseed. Flax seeds are one of the few vegetarian sources of omega-3 essential fatty acids and can be sprinkled over breakfast cereals and salads or mixed into breads and pastries.

HOW TO TOAST NUTS AND SEEDS

To remove the papery husk from hazelnuts or almonds, simply put the nuts on a baking sheet and heat in a preheated oven at 350°F/180°C for 5–10 minutes to loosen the skins. Remove, and when the nuts are cool enough to handle, rub off the skins in a clean dish towel.

Seeds and nuts, such as whole or slivered almonds, are also toasted to enhance their flavor. Smaller quantities of seeds can be toasted in a dry skillet until they change color, but for larger amounts, spread the seeds or nuts in a single layer on a baking sheet and roast in a preheated oven at 350°F/180°C for 5–7 minutes.

Herbs and Spices

Highly revered for thousands of years, herbs and spices can enliven even the simplest of meals. Invaluable ingredients in the vegetarian kitchen, they enhance the aroma and flavor of both savory and sweet dishes. Both also have a positive effect on the digestive system. Although the following concentrates on fresh herbs, dried can make a useful alternative, especially during the winter months when some fresh herbs are not available.

HERBS

Fresh herbs are now sold loose, in pots or packages. It is possible to enhance the shelf life of the latter by removing the herbs from the package and immersing the stems in a jar of water. Cover with a plastic bag, then seal with an elastic band; the herbs should keep for up to a week.

BASIL

Basil is a popular fresh herb and is commonly used in Italian dishes, especially pesto. The purple variety is widely used in Thai cooking. The fragile leaves are best torn rather than cut with a knife to prevent them bruising. Drying basil impairs its taste so is not recommended.

CILANTRO

Another favorite in Thai cooking, the warm and spicy flavor of cilantro also enlivens Indian dishes. The root is edible and can be ground into Indian and Thai curry pastes.

MINT

There are numerous varieties of mint; peppermint and spearmint being the most readily available. Mint can be mixed with plain yogurt to make raita, a calming accompaniment to hot curries; immersed in hot water to make a refreshing mint tea; or used in the fragrant salad, tabbouleh.

DILL

Dill is a scented herb. The featherlike leaves of the plant are used as a herb, while the seeds come from the flower heads after they have matured.

TARRAGON

Tarragon is popular in French cooking and has an affinity with egg and cheese dishes.

CHIVES

Chives are a part of the onion family, but have a milder flavor that works best when sprinkled over salads, eggs, and tomato-based dishes as a garnish.

BAY

The attractive, glossy green leaves of the bay tree add a robust, spicy flavor to stocks and stews, and are used to make bouquet garni.

OREGANO

Oregano is one of the few fresh herbs that dries well. Closely related to marjoram, but with a more robust flavor, oregano especially complements tomato-based dishes. Both oregano and thyme work well in marinades and are largely interchangeable in their uses.

PARSLEY

Both flat-leaf and curly leaf parsley are commonly available in stores. Flat-leaf looks similar to cilantro and is preferable in cooking to the curly type.

SAGE, ROSEMARY, AND THYME

Sage is pungent in flavor, but can work well with nut roasts, bakes, and stews. Rosemary has a strong and aromatic flavor and works best in hearty soups and stews. Thyme has a strong piquant or lemony flavor.

SPICES

Spices—the seeds, fruit, pods, bark, and buds of plants—should be bought in small quantities from a store with a regular turnover of stock. Aroma is the best indication of freshness, as this diminishes when a spice is stale. Store spices in airtight jars away from direct sunlight.

GINGER

Ginger has a warming, slightly peppery flavor that is quite different from the fresh root. It is used to flavor cakes, breads, and cookies, but is also added to curries, stews, and soups.

CARDAMOM

Pungent, warm, and aromatic, the spice known as cardamom is derived from several plants. It is sold as a seed pod or ground as a spice.

CUMIN AND CORIANDER

A key component in Middle Eastern, North African, and Indian cooking, cumin comes both ground and in whole seed form. Black seeds, also known as nigella, have a sweeter and milder flavor than the brown seeds. Ground coriander is used in much the same way as cumin, while the ivory-colored whole seeds are often used as a pickling spice as well as ground in curries and tagines.

CINNAMON, NUTMEG, AND CLOVES

These have a wonderfully warming flavor and are often used together in cakes, desserts, and cookies. Whole cinnamon sticks (quills) flavor curries, pilafs, and fruit compotes.

SAFFRON

Saffron is the world's most expensive spice. Made from the dried stigmas of *Crocus sativus*, only a tiny amount is required to add a distinctive flavor and a golden color to paella, stews, and milky desserts.

PEPPER

Pepper is undoubtedly the most widely used spice and comes in a multitude of colors—black, white, pink, and green. The spice not only adds its own flavor to dishes, but brings out the flavor of other ingredients.

CAYENNE AND PAPRIKA

Cayenne is a fiery spice that adds color and flavor to curries, soups, and stews. Paprika is milder and can be used more liberally. Both are said to be good for the circulation.

VANILLA

Vanilla beans provide a fragrant, mellow, sweet taste, with a rich, perfumed aroma. They are often used in sweet dishes.

HOW TO FREEZE HERBS

Herbs must be in perfect condition before they are frozen: anything stale, bruised, or contaminated will not be improved by freezing.

Wash the herbs carefully and shake dry. Lay out on paper towels to dry completely, then transfer to a tray and open freeze in a single layer. Once frozen, pack into small bags or boxes and use as required.

Alternatively, chop the washed and dried herbs (they will bruise and blacken if they are not dry) and pack into ice-cube trays to half fill. Top off with water and freeze. Drop the herb ice cubes into stews, soups, and casseroles for an instant herb seasoning.

Get Cooking

While most vegetables can be eaten raw, there are numerous cooking techniques to add interest and variety to vegetarian meals. You want to maximize flavor, color, and texture, while preserving as much of the essential vitamins and nutrients as possible. Since vegetables are so central to your diet, it pays to consider how best to cook them.

FRESHLY PREPARED...

The fresher the ingredients, the higher their nutrient content. Avoid old, tired, wilted vegetables and do not store anything for long at home. It is far better to buy fresh and loose when you need them, and to select organic if you can, in preference to ready-prepared packs, which will have lost some of their vitamins as well as their flavor. If possible, avoid peeling vegetables, because many nutrients are stored close to or in the skin (or put the peelings into a pot to make stock). Wash or scrub everything, but don't leave vegetables soaking in water or their soluble nutrients will leach out. Similarly, do not cut or prepare vegetables too far in advance, as some vitamins, such as vitamin C, diminish once the cut surface is exposed to the air.

BOILING

The traditional way to cook vegetables is to use plenty of salted water and a large, uncovered pan. This method is most suitable for corn, potatoes, and other root vegetables. Although steaming is preferable when cooking green vegetables because they retain more nutrients, if you choose to boil them leave them uncovered; put the lid on and they lose their attractive bright green color. Choose an appropriate-size pan for the amount of vegetables so that the water can circulate, but use the minimum amount of water, cook for the briefest period and drain the vegetables immediately, because boiling destroys water-soluble vitamins, such as B and C. Other soluble nutrients leach into the cooking water, so get into the habit of keeping the cooking water and use it as a base for soup or sauces.

right When boiling broccoli keep the lid off the pan to preserve the color.

POACHING

A less vigorous way to cook more delicate vegetables is to put them in boiling liquid (water, stock, wine, or milk), then to simmer them gently over low heat to retain their flavor, texture, and shape.

BRAISING

This cooking method requires only a very little water, and the pan is covered. The heat is much reduced and the cooking time greatly increased. You can start by browning the ingredients in a little oil or butter, then add water or other liquid before covering the pan. The small amount of liquid that remains at the end of cooking will be sweet and flavored—serve the vegetables with this juice and you gain all the nutrients. Onions, white turnips, leeks, chicory, celery, and fennel lend themselves to braising. Red cabbage is one of the brassicas that positively benefits from this long, slow treatment.

STEAMING

Unlike boiling, less water comes into contact with steamed vegetables, so they are crisper and retain more essential nutrients. Also, some vegetables—snow peas, leeks, and zucchini—become limp and unappetizing if boiled. Steamed new potatoes are particularly delicious; try putting some fresh mint leaves under the potatoes to flavor them while they are steaming.

COOKING TIMES

For maximum nutritional benefit, it makes sense to cook your vegetables for the least time possible. Cut them the same size so that they look attractive and cook evenly. While potatoes have to be cooked right through, other root vegetables, such as carrots, are best served with a little "bite" to them. Boil for less time or steam your vegetables and enjoy the extra crunch. Some vegetables—those with a high water content such as spinach, celery, or bean sprouts—need only be blanched in boiling water for 30 seconds.

For pan-frying or stir-frying, ensure that the oil is properly hot before adding the vegetables. When time is short, try microwaving your vegetables. This method requires less liquid or fat as well as shorter cooking times than conventional cooking.

below *When braising, brown the vegetables before adding only a little water and cook slowly.*

FRYING

Deep-frying is less popular these days, with concerns over the amount of fat in our diet. In fact, if the cooking temperature is correct, deep-fried foods are quickly sealed and absorb less oil than when they are pan-fried. Coating vegetables in batter or in egg and bread crumbs forms a crispy seal, which also reduces oil absorption. Deep-frying is a long-established cooking method for potatoes (french fries) and also works well for eggplants and zucchini. Dry-frying in a skillet or in a stovetop ridged grill pan or on a flat griddle plate is a healthier option that can be used for some vegetables as well as halloumi or provolone cheese.

left *Roast vegetables in a roasting tin with olive oil and herbs to add extra flavor.*

below *Sautée slowly in an uncovered skillet, using only a little olive oil to cook the vegetables.*

STIR-FRYING

This method of frying in a little oil over very high heat has become widely popular. Stir-fried vegetables retain far more of their nutritional value, flavor, texture, and color. Typically, vegetables are very thinly sliced and rapidly moved around in a hot wok to aid fast and even cooking. Most of us are familiar with stir-fried baby corn, snowpeas, bell peppers, bean sprouts, and bamboo shoots, but the method is an equally good way to cook thinly sliced cauliflower, Brussels sprouts, cabbage, and carrots.

ROASTING

Traditionally, roasting vegetables meant cooking them in the fat dripping from a joint of meat. A far healthier vegetarian option is to roast vegetables lightly drizzled with olive oil in a roasting pan, to which you can add garlic and herbs for additional flavor. Roast squash, parsnips, onions, tomatoes, asparagus and even beet are all delicious; the flavor is concentrated and the natural sweetness accentuated.

SAUTÉEING AND SWEATING

These methods use less oil than traditional pan frying and are longer, slower processes than stir-frying. Sautéeing is done in an uncovered skillet; sweating in either a heavy-bottomed casserole or skillet, covered, so that water from the ingredients is trapped and falls back into the pan. Onions are often sweated to soften but not color.

BAKING

Potatoes, onions, and garlic can be baked "dry" in their skins, while softer vegetables (bell peppers and tomatoes) can be stuffed with rice and other fillings or foil-wrapped.

BROILING AND BARBECUING

The intense heat from a broiler or charcoal is unsuitable for either delicate or dense vegetables, which only become charred not cooked, but excellent for softer ones, such as onions, corn, eggplants, and tomatoes. All vegetables need to be brushed with oil before being placed on the barbecue.

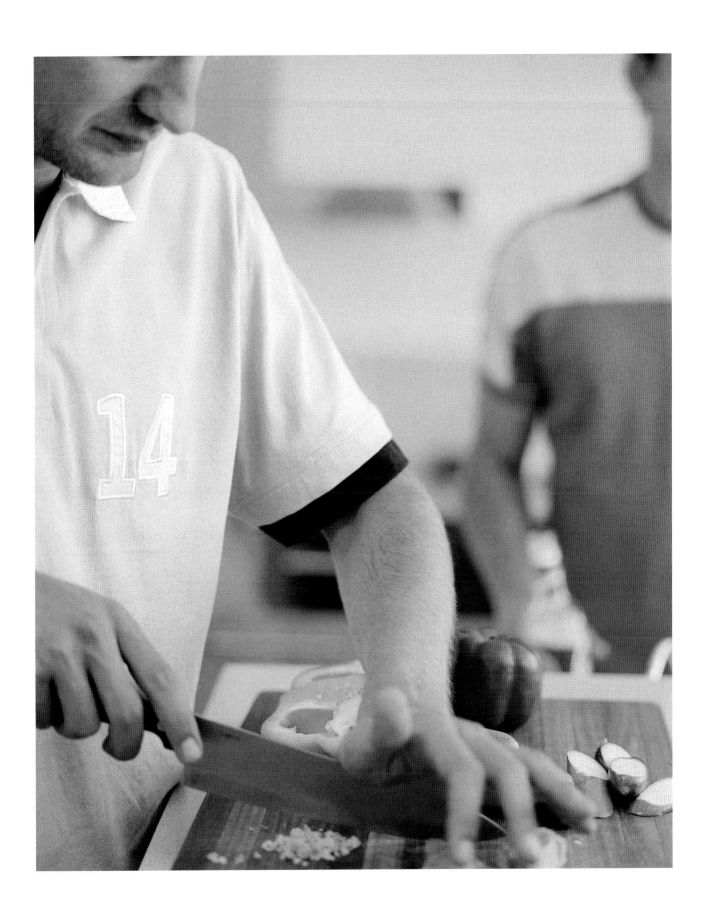

Basic Recipes

The recipes in this book provide a wide variety of delicious vegetarian meals. Some of them incorporate a common basic recipe, to which you can refer on these pages, or you can use these basic recipes as an addition to a dish of your choice.

CHEESE SAUCE
Makes: 2½ cups

VEGETABLE STOCK
Makes: 8½ cups

2 tbsp sunflower-seed or corn oil
4 oz/115 g onions, finely chopped
4 oz/115 g leeks, finely chopped
4 oz/115 g carrots, finely chopped
4 celery stalks, finely chopped
3 oz/85 g fennel, finely chopped
3 oz/85 g tomatoes, finely chopped
9½ cups water
1 bouquet garni

Heat the oil in a large pan over low heat. Add the onions and leeks and cook, stirring frequently, for 5 minutes, or until softened.

Add the remaining vegetables, cover, and cook over very low heat, stirring occasionally, for 10 minutes. Add the water and bouquet garni and bring to a boil, then reduce the heat and let simmer for 20 minutes.

Strain, let cool, then cover and store in the refrigerator. Use within 3 days or freeze in portions for up to 3 months.

3 tbsp butter
5 tbsp all-purpose flour
2½ cups milk
1¼ cups grated Cheddar cheese
salt and pepper

Melt the butter in a pan over medium heat. Stir in the flour and cook, stirring constantly, for 1–2 minutes.

Remove from the heat and gradually whisk in the milk. Return to the heat and bring to a boil, whisking constantly. Let simmer for 2 minutes, or until the sauce is thick and glossy. Remove from the heat, add the cheese, and stir until melted. Season to taste with salt and pepper.

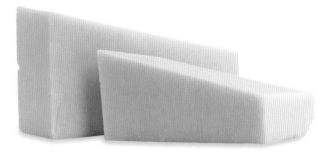

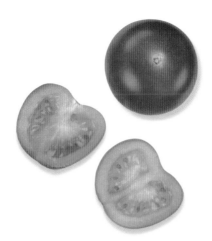

TOMATO SAUCE

Makes: ⅔ cup

1 tbsp olive oil
1 small onion, chopped
1 garlic clove, chopped
14 oz/400 g canned chopped
  tomatoes
2 tbsp chopped fresh parsley
1 tsp dried oregano
2 bay leaves
2 tbsp tomato paste
1 tsp sugar
salt and pepper

Heat the oil in a pan over medium heat. Add the onion and cook, stirring, for 2–3 minutes until beginning to soften.

Add the garlic and cook, stirring, for 1 minute. Stir in the tomatoes, parsley, oregano, bay leaves, tomato paste, and sugar, and season to taste with salt and pepper.

Bring the sauce to a boil, then reduce the heat and let simmer, uncovered, for 15–20 minutes until the sauce has reduced by half. Remove and discard the bay leaves just before serving.

MAYONNAISE

Makes: 1¼ cups

2 egg yolks
pinch of salt, plus extra for seasoning
⅔ cup sunflower-seed or corn oil
⅔ cup olive oil
1 tbsp white wine vinegar
2 tsp Dijon mustard
pepper

Beat the egg yolks with the pinch of salt in a bowl.

Whisk the oils together in a pitcher. Gradually add one quarter of the oil mixture to the egg yolks, a drop at a time, beating constantly with a whisk or electric mixer.

Beat in the vinegar, then continue adding the oils in a steady stream, beating constantly.

Once all the oil has been incorporated, stir in the mustard and season to taste with salt and pepper.

PESTO SAUCE

Makes: ⅓ cup

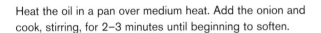

2 oz/55 g fresh basil
  leaves
⅛ cup pine nuts
1 garlic clove
pinch of salt
¼ cup freshly grated Parmesan cheese
3 tbsp extra virgin olive oil

Put the basil leaves, pine nuts, garlic, and salt in a mortar and pound to a paste with a pestle.

Transfer to a bowl and, with a wooden spoon, gradually work in the Parmesan cheese, followed by the oil, to make a thick, creamy sauce.

Cover with plastic wrap and refrigerate until required.

TZATZIKI
Makes: generous 2 cups

generous 2 cups strained plain yogurt or other
  thick plain yogurt
4 garlic cloves, very finely chopped
2 cucumbers, peeled, seeded, and very finely diced
1 tbsp lemon-flavored or extra virgin olive oil
3 tbsp lemon juice
1 tbsp chopped fresh mint leaves
salt and pepper
paprika, to garnish

TO SERVE
celery sticks
carrot sticks
pita bread triangles

Put the yogurt, garlic, cucumber, oil, lemon juice, and mint in a serving bowl and stir together until well combined. Season to taste with salt and pepper, cover with plastic wrap, and let chill in the refrigerator for at least 2 hours, or until required.

When ready to use, garnish with a little paprika. Serve with celery and carrot sticks and pita bread triangles for dipping.

RICH SHORTCRUST PIE DOUGH
Makes: 1 x 9-inch/23-cm tart

1⅜ cups all-purpose flour
pinch of salt
6 tbsp butter, diced, plus extra for greasing
1 egg yolk
3 tbsp ice-cold water

Sift the flour with the salt into a bowl. Add the butter and rub into the flour with your fingertips until the mixture resembles fine bread crumbs.

Beat the egg yolk with the water in a small bowl. Sprinkle the liquid over the flour mixture and combine with a round-bladed knife or your fingertips to form a dough. Shape the dough into a ball, wrap in foil, and chill in the refrigerator for 30 minutes.

PUFF PASTRY

Makes: 1 x 10-inch/25-cm tart or pie

1⅜ cups all-purpose flour, plus extra for dusting
pinch of salt
¾ cup unsalted butter
about ⅔ cup ice-cold water

Sift the flour with the salt into a large bowl. Dice 2 tablespoons of the butter and rub into the flour with your fingertips. Gradually add the water, just enough to bring the dough together, and knead briefly to form a smooth dough. Wrap in foil and chill in the refrigerator for 30 minutes.

Keep the remaining butter out of the refrigerator, wrap in foil, and shape into a 1¼-inch/3-cm thick rectangle. Roll out the dough on a lightly floured counter to a rectangle 3 times longer and 1¼ inches/3 cm wider than the butter, unwrap the butter and put in the center of the dough, long-side toward you. Fold over the 2 "wings" of dough to enclose the butter, press down the edges with the rolling pin to seal, and then turn the dough so that the short side faces you. Roll out the dough to its original length, fold into 3, turn, and roll again to its original length.

Repeat this once more, then rewrap the dough and chill again for 30 minutes. Repeat the rolling and turning twice more. Chill again for 30 minutes. At this point you can freeze the dough until you need it.

PIZZA DOUGH BASES

Makes: 2 x 10-inch/25-cm pizzas

1⅔ cups all-purpose flour, plus extra for dusting
1 tsp salt
6 tbsp lukewarm water
2 tbsp olive oil, plus extra for oiling
1 tsp active dry yeast

Sift the flour with the salt into a large, warmed bowl and make a well in the center. Add the water, oil, and yeast to the well. Using a wooden spoon or your hands, gradually mix in, drawing the flour from the side, to form a dough.

Turn out onto a lightly floured counter and knead for 5 minutes, or until smooth and elastic. Form the dough into a ball, put in a clean, lightly oiled bowl, and cover with oiled plastic wrap. Leave in a warm place to rise for 1 hour, or until doubled in size.

Turn out the dough onto a lightly floured counter and knock back. Knead briefly before shaping into 2 pizza bases.

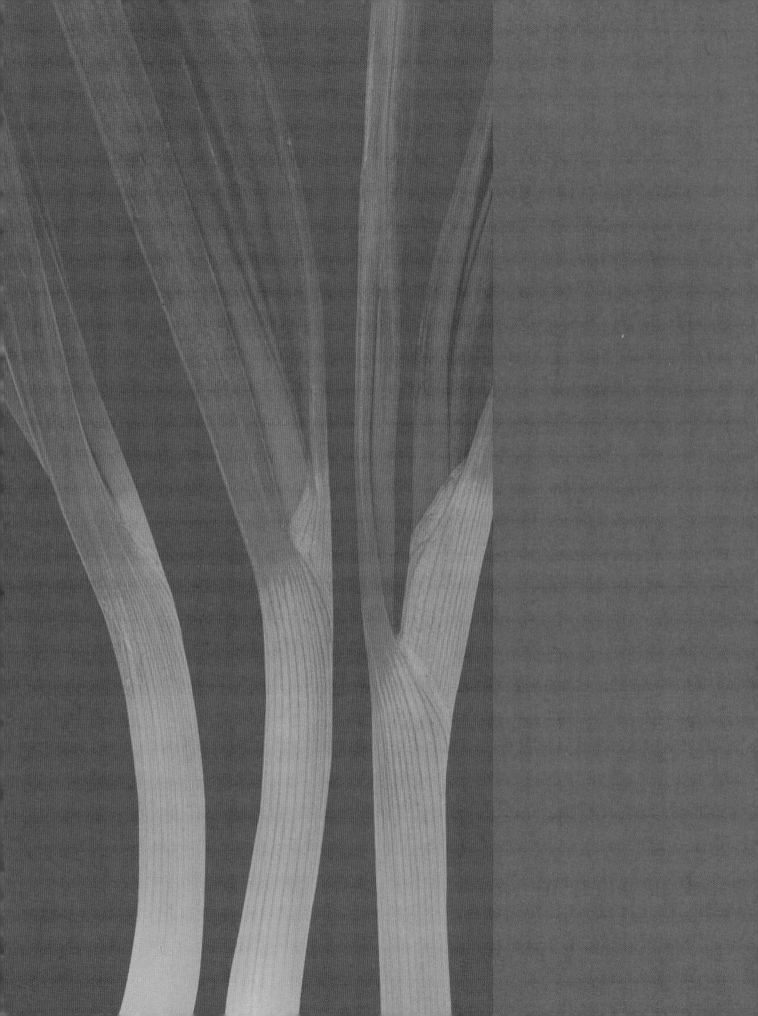

2

Homemade soups provide a powerhouse of nutrients as well as a wealth of flavors, and you can be sure that they aren't overloaded with salt, unlike so many of even the better-quality commercially produced varieties. What's more, they are surprisingly quick and easy to make.

SOUPS

Whether you want a soup that's hearty and chunky or something more luxurious and smooth, perhaps a light, fragrant broth as a prelude to an Asian-style meal or even a chilled soup, you are sure to find a recipe to fit the bill. The collection includes such great vegetarian classics as Vichyssoise, Gazpacho, French Onion Soup, and Bortsch.

serves 6 | prep 40 mins, plus 4–8 hrs' chilling | cook 35 mins

vichyssoise

INGREDIENTS
1 lb/450 g leeks, white parts only
1 lb/450 g potatoes
4 tbsp butter
5 cups water
2½ cups milk
1¼ cups sour cream, plus extra
  to garnish
salt and pepper
2 tbsp snipped fresh chives, to garnish

Thinly slice the leeks. Peel and dice the potatoes. Melt the butter in a large, heavy-bottom pan over very low heat. Add the leeks, cover, and cook, stirring occasionally, for 10 minutes.

Stir in the potatoes and cook over medium heat, stirring frequently, for 2 minutes. Pour in the water and add a pinch of salt. Bring to a boil, then reduce the heat and let simmer for 15–20 minutes until the potatoes are tender. Remove from the heat and let cool slightly. Transfer to a blender or food processor and process into a purée. Push the mixture through a strainer into a clean pan with a wooden spoon, then stir in the milk. Season to taste with salt and pepper and stir in half the sour cream.

Reheat the soup, then push through a strainer into a bowl. Stir in the remaining cream, cover with plastic wrap, and let cool. Chill in the refrigerator for 4–8 hours. Serve in chilled bowls, with swirls of sour cream and chives to garnish.

COOK'S TIP

For a more intense flavor, you can use a vegetable bouillon powder or bouillon cube mixed with the water.

serves 4–6 | prep 20 mins, plus 4 hrs' chilling | No cooking required

gazpacho

INGREDIENTS
1 lb 2 oz/500 g large, juicy tomatoes, peeled, seeded, and chopped

3 large, ripe red bell peppers, cored, seeded, and chopped

2 tbsp sherry vinegar, or to taste

4 tbsp olive oil

pinch of sugar

salt and pepper

TO SERVE
ice cubes

finely diced red bell pepper

finely diced green bell pepper

finely diced yellow bell pepper

finely diced seeded cucumber

finely chopped hard-cooked eggs

croutons fried in garlic-flavored olive oil

COOK'S TIP
Flavors are dulled at cold temperatures so more seasoning will be needed than for a soup served warm. For this reason, taste and adjust the seasoning after chilling the soup.

Put the tomatoes, chopped bell peppers, vinegar, oil, and sugar in a blender or food processor and process until blended and as smooth or chunky as you like. Transfer to a bowl, cover, and let chill for at least 4 hours before serving. Taste and adjust the seasoning, adding extra vinegar, if necessary.

To serve, ladle the soup into bowls and add 1–2 ice cubes to each. Put the other accompaniments in bowls and let everyone add their own.

serves 3–4 | prep 5 mins, plus 4 hrs' chilling | cook 5 mins

chilled pea soup

INGREDIENTS
scant 2 cups vegetable stock or water
1 lb/450 g frozen peas
2 oz/55 g scallions, chopped, plus extra
  to garnish
1¼ cups plain yogurt or light cream
salt and pepper

TO GARNISH
2 tbsp chopped fresh mint or snipped fresh chives
grated lemon rind

Bring the stock to a boil in a large pan over medium heat. Reduce the heat, add the peas and scallions, and let simmer for 5 minutes.

Let cool slightly, then strain twice, making sure that you remove and discard any pieces of skin. Pour into a large bowl, season to taste with salt and pepper, and stir in the yogurt. Cover the bowl with plastic wrap and let chill in the refrigerator for several hours.

To serve, mix the soup well and ladle into a large tureen or individual soup bowls or mugs. Garnish with chopped mint or snipped chives, scallions, and grated lemon rind.

serves 6 | prep 30 mins | cook 1½ hrs

french onion soup

INGREDIENTS

1 lb 8 oz/675 g onions

3 tbsp olive oil

**4 garlic cloves, 3 chopped and
1 peeled but kept whole**

1 tsp sugar

**2 tsp chopped fresh thyme, plus extra sprigs
to garnish**

2 tbsp all-purpose flour

½ cup dry white wine

8½ cups vegetable stock

6 slices French bread

10½ oz/300 g Gruyère cheese, grated

Thinly slice the onions. Heat the oil in a large, heavy-bottom pan over medium–low heat, add the onions, and cook, stirring occasionally, for 10 minutes, or until they are just beginning to brown. Stir in the chopped garlic, sugar, and chopped thyme, then reduce the heat and cook, stirring occasionally, for 30 minutes, or until the onions are golden brown.

Sprinkle in the flour and cook, stirring constantly, for 1–2 minutes. Stir in the wine. Gradually stir in the stock and bring to a boil, skimming off any scum that rises to the surface, then reduce the heat and let simmer for 45 minutes. Meanwhile, preheat the broiler to medium–hot. Toast the bread on both sides under the broiler, then rub the toast with the whole garlic clove.

Ladle the soup into 6 ovenproof bowls set on a baking sheet. Float a piece of toast in each bowl and divide the grated cheese between them. Place under the broiler for 2–3 minutes, or until the cheese has just melted. Garnish with thyme sprigs and serve immediately.

VARIATION

If desired, you can stir 2 tablespoons brandy into the soup just before ladling it into the bowls.

COOK'S TIP

Make sure that you allow yourself plenty of time to make the vegetable stock in advance of making the soup. If the stock is left to stand, the flavors will have time to develop.

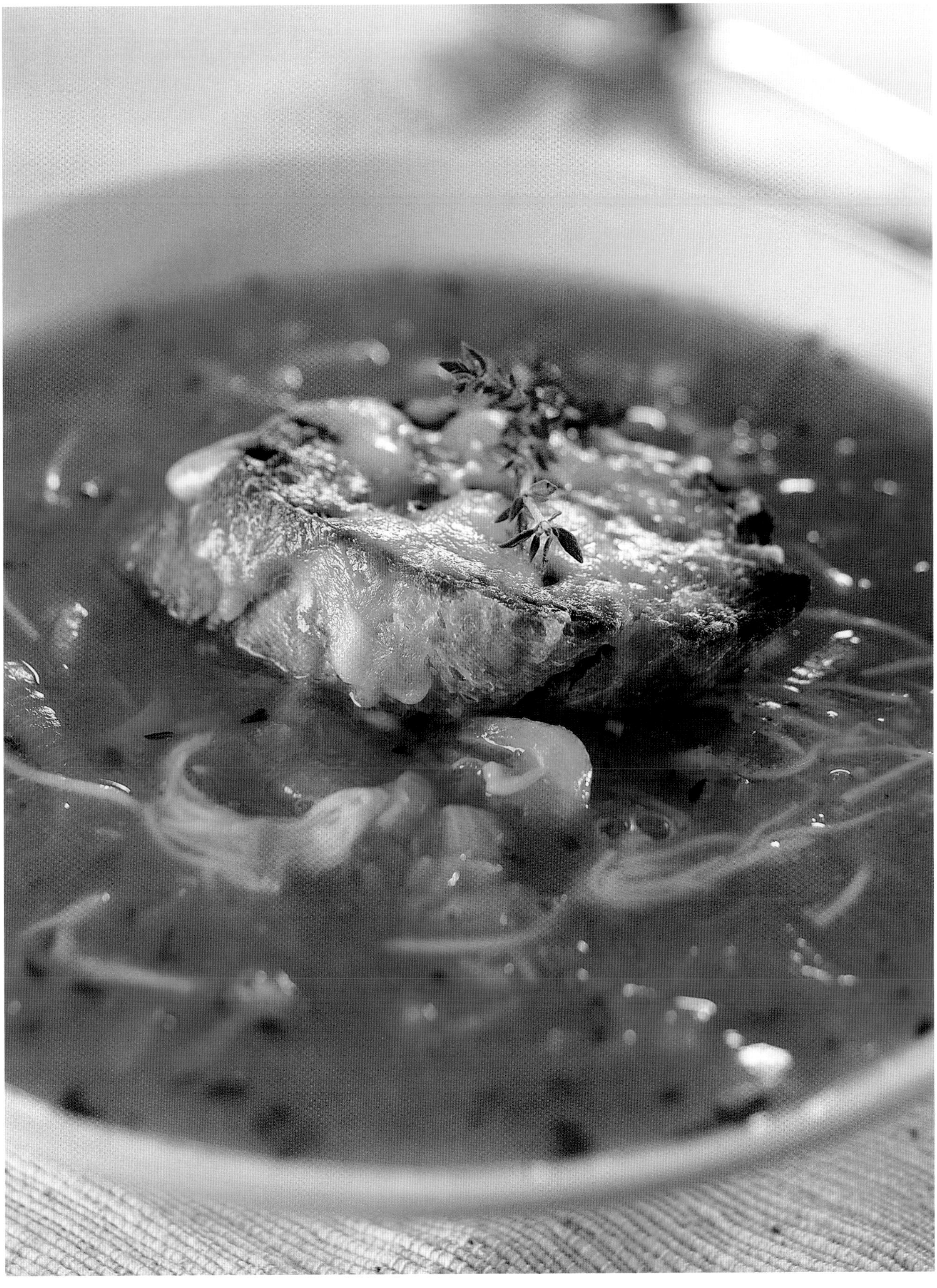

serves 8 | prep 30 mins, plus 4 mins' standing | cook 1 hr 40 mins

genoese vegetable soup

INGREDIENTS

2 onions, sliced

2 carrots, diced

2 celery stalks, sliced

2 potatoes, peeled and diced

4 oz/115 g green beans, cut into
  1-inch/2.5-cm lengths

1 cup peas, thawed if frozen

4⅜ cups fresh spinach leaves, coarse stems
  removed, shredded

2 zucchini, diced

8 oz/225 g Italian plum tomatoes, peeled,
  seeded, and diced

3 garlic cloves, thinly sliced

4 tbsp extra virgin olive oil

8½ cups vegetable stock

1 quantity pesto sauce

5 oz/140 g dried stellete or other soup pasta

salt and pepper

freshly grated Parmesan cheese, to serve

COOK'S TIP

*To peel tomatoes, cut a
cross in the base of each
and put in a heatproof bowl.
Cover with boiling water and
let stand for 30–45 seconds.
Drain and plunge into cold
water, then the skins will
slide off easily.*

Put the onions, carrots, celery, potatoes, beans, peas, spinach, zucchini, tomatoes, and garlic in a large, heavy-bottom pan over medium–low heat, pour in the extra virgin olive oil and stock, and bring to a boil. Reduce the heat and let simmer gently, stirring occasionally, for 1½ hours.

Meanwhile, make the pesto sauce. Cover with plastic wrap and refrigerate until required.

Season the soup to taste with salt and pepper and add the pasta. Cook for an additional 8–10 minutes until the pasta is tender but still firm to the bite. The soup should be very thick.

Stir in half the pesto sauce, remove from the heat, and let stand for 4 minutes. Taste and adjust the seasoning, adding more salt, pepper, and pesto sauce, if necessary. (Any leftover pesto sauce may be stored in a screw-top jar in the refrigerator for up to 2 weeks.)

Ladle into warmed bowls and serve immediately. Hand round the extra Parmesan cheese separately.

serves 4 | prep 20 mins | cook 10 mins

chinese vegetable soup

INGREDIENTS

4 oz/115 g Napa cabbage
2 tbsp peanut oil
8 oz/225 g firm marinated tofu, cut into
½-inch/1-cm cubes
2 garlic cloves, thinly sliced
4 scallions, thinly sliced diagonally
1 carrot, thinly sliced
4 cups vegetable stock
1 tbsp Chinese rice wine
2 tbsp light soy sauce
1 tsp sugar
salt and pepper

Shred the Napa cabbage and set aside. Heat the oil in a large preheated wok or skillet over high heat. Add the tofu cubes and stir-fry for 4–5 minutes until browned. Remove from the wok with a slotted spoon and drain on paper towels.

Add the garlic, scallions, and carrot to the wok and stir-fry for 2 minutes. Pour in the stock, rice wine, and soy sauce, then add the sugar and shredded Napa cabbage. Cook over medium heat, stirring, for an additional 1–2 minutes until heated through.

Season to taste with salt and pepper and return the tofu to the wok. Ladle the soup into warmed bowls and serve.

VARIATION

If you are unable to find Chinese rice wine, substitute dry sherry. You can also use firm lettuce leaves, such as Boston or romaine, instead of Napa cabbage.

serves 4 | prep 10 mins, plus 1 hr soaking | cook 5 mins

hot-&-sour soup

INGREDIENTS

6 dried shiitake mushrooms

4 oz/115 g dried rice vermicelli noodles

4 small fresh green chilies, seeded
and chopped

6 tbsp rice wine vinegar

3½ cups vegetable stock

2 lemon grass stalks, snapped in half

4 oz/115 g canned water chestnuts, drained,
rinsed, and halved

6 tbsp Thai soy sauce

juice of 1 lime

1 tbsp jaggery or brown sugar

3 scallions, chopped, to garnish

Put the dried mushrooms in a heatproof bowl and pour in enough boiling water to cover. Set aside to soak for 1 hour. Meanwhile, put the noodles in a separate heatproof bowl and pour in enough boiling water to cover. Set aside to soak for 10 minutes. Combine the chilies and vinegar in a third bowl and set aside.

Drain the mushrooms and noodles. Bring the stock to a boil in a large pan over high heat. Add the mushrooms, noodles, lemon grass, water chestnuts, soy sauce, lime juice, and sugar and return to a boil.

Stir in the chili and vinegar mixture and cook for 1–2 minutes. Remove and discard the lemon grass. Ladle the soup into warmed bowls and serve hot, garnished with scallions.

serves 4–6 | prep 10 mins | cook 40 mins

tomato soup

INGREDIENTS
2 lb/900 g large, juicy tomatoes, halved
2 tbsp butter
1 tbsp olive oil
1 large onion, sliced
2–3 tbsp tomato paste, depending on the
flavor of the tomatoes
3 cups vegetable stock
2 tbsp amontillado sherry
½ tsp sugar
salt and pepper
crusty bread, to serve

TO GARNISH
parsley, chopped
⅔ cup light cream (optional)

COOK'S TIP
If you don't possess a mouli,
purée the soup in a blender
or food processor, then work
through a fine strainer to
achieve the smooth texture.

Preheat the broiler to high. Put the tomatoes, cut-sides up, on a baking sheet and broil about 4 inches/10 cm from the heat for 5 minutes, or until just starting to char on the edges.

Meanwhile, melt the butter with the oil in a large pan or ovenproof casserole over medium heat. Add the onion and cook, stirring frequently, for 5 minutes. Stir in the tomato paste and cook for an additional 2 minutes.

Add the tomatoes, stock, sherry, sugar, and salt and pepper to taste to the pan and stir. Bring to a boil, then reduce the heat to low and let simmer, covered, for 20 minutes, or until the tomatoes are reduced to a pulp.

Process the soup through a mouli into a large bowl. Return to the rinsed-out pan and let simmer, uncovered, for 10 minutes, or until the desired consistency is achieved. Ladle into individual bowls. Cool and serve chilled, if desired, decorating with swirls of cream and garnishing with parsley. Serve with plenty of bread.

serves 4 | prep 20 mins | cook 15 mins

corn, potato & cheese soup

INGREDIENTS
2 tbsp butter
2 shallots, finely chopped
8 oz/225 g potatoes, peeled and diced
4 tbsp all-purpose flour
2 tbsp dry white wine
1¼ cups milk
11½ oz/325 g canned corn kernels, drained
3 oz/85 g Gruyère, Emmental, or
  Cheddar cheese, grated
8–10 fresh sage leaves, chopped, plus extra
  sprigs to garnish
scant 2 cups heavy cream

CROUTONS
2–3 slices day-old white bread
2 tbsp olive oil

To make the croutons, cut the crusts off the bread slices, then cut the bread into ¼-inch/5-mm squares. Heat the oil in a heavy-bottom skillet over high heat, add the bread cubes, and cook, tossing and stirring constantly, until evenly colored. Remove with a slotted spoon, drain thoroughly on paper towels, and set aside.

Melt the butter in a large, heavy-bottom pan over low heat. Add the shallots and cook, stirring frequently, for 5 minutes, or until softened. Add the potatoes and cook, stirring, for 2 minutes.

Sprinkle in the flour and cook, stirring constantly, for 1 minute. Remove from the heat and stir in the wine, then return to the heat and gradually stir in the milk. Bring to a boil, stirring constantly, then reduce the heat to a simmer.

Stir in the corn, cheese, chopped sage, and cream and heat through gently until the cheese has just melted. Ladle the soup into warmed bowls and sprinkle over the croutons. Garnish with sage sprigs and serve immediately.

COOK'S TIP
When you are cooking croutons, make sure that the oil is very hot before adding the bread cubes, otherwise the cubes may turn out soggy rather than crisp.

serves 4 | prep 15 mins | cook 40 mins

hearty lentil & vegetable soup

INGREDIENTS
2 tbsp vegetable oil
3 leeks, green parts included, finely sliced
3 carrots, diced
2 celery stalks, quartered lengthwise and diced
generous 1 cup brown or green lentils
generous ⅓ cup long-grain rice
4 cups vegetable stock
8 fresh corncob quarters
salt and pepper

TO GARNISH
4 tbsp snipped fresh chives
⅔ cup sour cream

Heat the oil in a large pan over medium heat. Add the leeks, carrots, and celery, cover, and cook, stirring occasionally, for 5–7 minutes until just tender. Stir in the lentils and rice.

Stir in the stock. Bring to a boil, then reduce the heat, cover, and let simmer over medium–low heat for 20 minutes. Add the corncobs and let simmer, covered, for an additional 10 minutes, or until the lentils and rice are tender.

Season the soup to taste with salt and pepper. Ladle into individual warmed bowls, sprinkle with chives, and top with a spoonful of sour cream. Serve immediately.

serves 6 | prep 30 mins | cook 1¼ hrs

bortsch

INGREDIENTS

1 onion

4 tbsp butter

12 oz/350 g raw beet, cut into thin sticks, and 1 raw beet, grated

1 carrot, cut into thin sticks

3 celery stalks, thinly sliced

2 tomatoes, peeled, seeded, and chopped

6 cups vegetable stock

1 tbsp white wine vinegar

1 tbsp sugar

2 large fresh dill sprigs, including to garnish

4 oz/115 g white cabbage, shredded

salt and pepper

⅔ cup sour cream, to garnish

rye bread, to serve (optional)

COOK'S TIP

It is not essential to add extra beet toward the end of cooking, but this helps to provide the spectacular purple color of the soup and also freshens the flavor.

Slice the onion into rings. Melt the butter in a large, heavy-bottom pan over low heat. Add the onion and cook, stirring frequently, for 5 minutes until softened. Add the beet sticks, carrot, celery, and tomatoes and cook, stirring frequently, for 4–5 minutes.

Snip the dill sprigs. Add the stock, vinegar, sugar, and a tablespoon of dill into the pan. Season to taste with salt and pepper. Bring to a boil, then reduce the heat and let simmer for 35–40 minutes until the vegetables are tender.

Stir in the cabbage, cover, and let simmer for an additional 10 minutes. Stir in the grated beet, with any juices, and cook for an additional 10 minutes. Ladle into warmed bowls. Garnish with a spoonful of sour cream and another tablespoon of snipped dill and serve with rye bread, if desired.

VARIATION

For a more substantial soup, add 2 diced potatoes with the cabbage to the pan. Cook for an additional 10 minutes before adding the grated beet.

serves 4 | prep 15 mins | cook 25–30 mins

watercress soup

INGREDIENTS

**2 bunches of watercress, about 7 oz/200 g,
  thoroughly washed**
1½ tbsp butter
2 onions, chopped
8 oz/225 g potatoes, peeled and coarsely chopped
5 cups vegetable stock or water
whole nutmeg, for grating (optional)
½ cup crème fraîche or sour cream, to garnish
salt and pepper

Remove the leaves from the stalks of the watercress and set side. Coarsely chop the stalks.

Melt the butter in a large pan over medium heat, add the onion, and cook, stirring frequently, for 4–5 minutes until softened but not browned.

Add the potatoes and mix well with the onion. Stir in the watercress stalks and stock.

Bring to a boil, then reduce the heat, cover, and let simmer for 15–20 minutes until the potato is tender.

Stir in the watercress leaves and heat through. Remove from the heat and let cool slightly. Using a hand-held stick blender, blend the soup until smooth, or transfer to a blender or food processor and process until smooth. Return to the rinsed-out pan.

Reheat the soup, season to taste with salt and pepper, and add a generous grating of nutmeg, if desired. Serve in warmed bowls with the crème fraîche spooned on top.

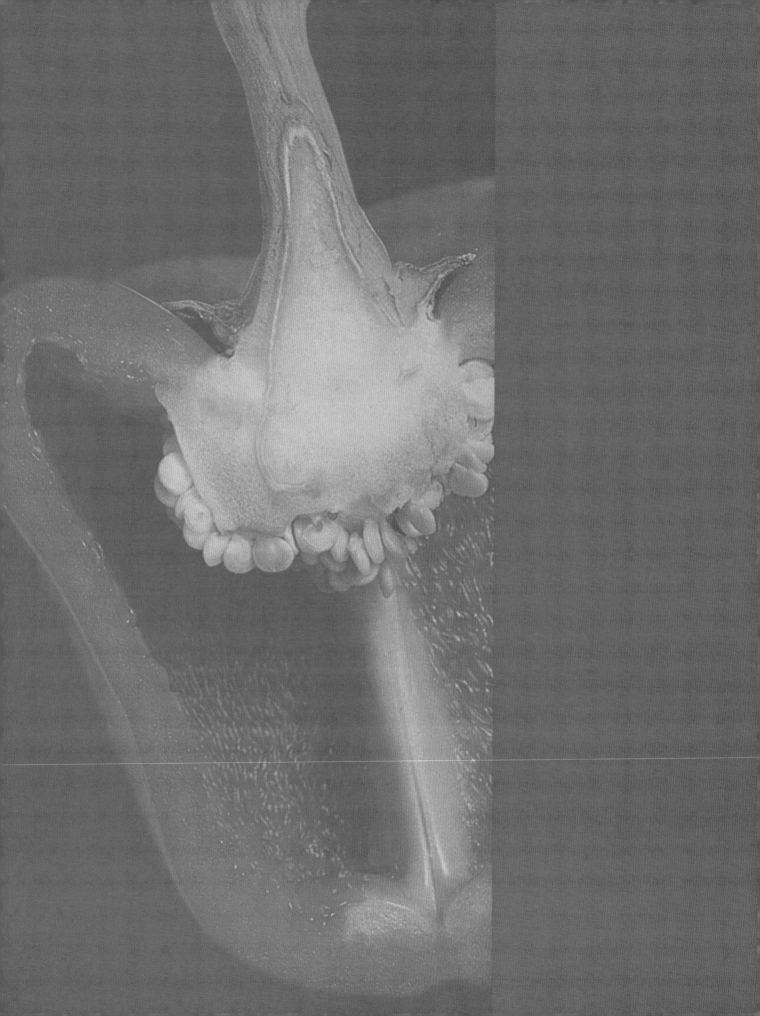

3

Color and texture abound in this enticing range of recipes, which exploit to the full those characteristic virtues of what we still consider essentially Mediterranean vegetables, such as eggplants, zucchini, bell peppers, and sun-dried tomatoes, flavored with garlic, basil, and oregano.

APPETIZERS & LIGHT MEALS

There are other culinary influences to sample and savor, however, from fiery Mexican Vegetable Fajitas to Chinese-style Sweet-&-Sour Vegetables with Cashews. You can also indulge in some comfort-food favorites, including creamy Cauliflower Cheese, Indian-spiced Bean Burgers, and crisp-baked Potato Skins with Tomato & Corn Salsa.

serves 4 | prep 20 mins, plus 9½ hrs' marinating | cook 15 mins

antipasti

INGREDIENTS
1 lb/450 g large mushrooms
5 garlic cloves
about 1¾ cups extra virgin olive oil
1 tbsp finely chopped fresh rosemary
1 cup dry white wine
3 red bell peppers
3 orange bell peppers
4 tbsp fresh basil leaves
pinch of chili powder
grated rind of 1 lemon
1⅓ cups black olives
2 tbsp chopped fresh parsley
salt and pepper

Slice the mushrooms and put in a large serving dish. Chop 1 garlic clove. Heat 4 tablespoons of the oil in a small pan over medium heat. Add the chopped garlic, rosemary, and wine and bring to a boil. Reduce the heat and let simmer for 3 minutes. Season to taste with salt and pepper. Pour the wine mixture over the mushrooms. Let cool, stirring occasionally. Cover with plastic wrap and let marinate in the refrigerator for 8 hours.

Meanwhile, preheat the broiler to medium–high. Cook the bell peppers under the broiler, turning frequently, until the skins are blackened. Transfer to a bowl, cover, and let cool, then peel, halve, and seed. Cut the flesh into strips. Put in a clean serving dish. Slice the remaining garlic and add to the dish with the basil. Season to taste with salt, add enough of the remaining oil to cover, and toss lightly. Cover with plastic wrap and let marinate in the refrigerator for 8 hours.

Meanwhile, heat the remaining oil, or about ½ cup, in a pan over low heat. Add the chili powder and lemon rind and cook, stirring, for 2 minutes. Add the olives and cook, stirring, for 1 minute. Transfer to a clean serving dish, sprinkle with the parsley, and let cool. Cover and let marinate in the refrigerator for at least 8 hours. Remove the antipasti from the refrigerator 1 hour before serving.

COOK'S TIP
Plan to make these antipasti a day before you will need them. This way, you can leave the dishes to marinate in the refrigerator overnight.

serves 4 | prep 15 mins | cook 10 mins

felafel with tahini sauce

INGREDIENTS
1 lb/450 g canned cannellini beans, drained
12 oz/350 g canned chickpeas, drained
1 onion, finely chopped
2 garlic cloves, chopped
1 small fresh red chili, seeded and chopped
1 tsp baking powder
1 oz/25 g fresh parsley, chopped, plus extra
  sprigs to garnish
pinch of cayenne
2 tbsp water
vegetable oil, for deep-frying
salt and pepper

TAHINI SAUCE
scant 1 cup sesame seed paste
1 garlic clove, chopped
1–2 tbsp water
2–3 tsp lemon juice

TO SERVE
pita bread
thick plain yogurt or tzatziki
lemon wedges

To make the tahini sauce, put the sesame seed paste and garlic in a bowl. Gradually stir in the water until a fairly smooth consistency is reached, then stir in lemon juice to taste. Add more water or lemon juice, if necessary. Cover with plastic wrap and let chill in the refrigerator until required.

To make the felafel, rinse and drain the beans and chickpeas. Put them in a food processor with the onion, garlic, chili, baking powder, chopped parsley, and cayenne pepper. Process to a coarse paste, then add the water and season with plenty of salt and pepper. Process again briefly.

Heat about 2½ inches/6 cm of oil in a deep-fat fryer, large, heavy-bottom pan, or wok over high heat. Deep-fry rounded tablespoonfuls of the mixture in batches for 2–2½ minutes until golden and crispy on the outside. Remove with a slotted spoon and drain well on paper towels. Serve hot or cold, garnished with parsley sprigs and accompanied by the tahini sauce, pita bread, yogurt or tzatziki, and lemon wedges.

serves 4 | prep 10 mins | cook 10 mins

cheese & sun-dried tomato toasts

INGREDIENTS
2 sfilatini loaves
¾ cup sun-dried tomato paste
10½ oz/300 g mozzarella di bufala, drained
and diced
1½ tsp dried oregano
2–3 tbsp olive oil
pepper

Preheat the broiler to high and preheat the oven to 425°F/220°C. Slice the loaves diagonally and discard the end pieces. Toast the slices on both sides under the broiler until golden.

Spread one side of each toast with the sun-dried tomato paste and top with mozzarella. Sprinkle with oregano and season to taste with pepper.

Put the toasts on a large baking sheet and drizzle with oil. Bake in the preheated oven for 5 minutes, or until the cheese is melted and bubbling. Remove the toasts from the oven and let stand for 5 minutes before serving.

COOK'S TIP
If you are unable to find
sfilatini, use a large ciabatta
loaf instead and cut the
slices in half.

serves 4 | prep 15 mins | cook 20–30 mins

stuffed eggplants

INGREDIENTS
8 small eggplants
2 tbsp vegetable or peanut oil
4 shallots, finely chopped
2 garlic cloves, crushed
2 fresh red chilies, seeded and chopped
1 zucchini, coarsely chopped
4 oz/115 g creamed coconut, chopped
few fresh Thai basil leaves, chopped
small handful of fresh cilantro, chopped
4 tbsp Thai soy sauce

TO SERVE
rice with chopped scallions
sweet chili sauce

Preheat the oven to 400°F/200°C. Put the eggplants in a roasting pan and cook in the preheated oven for 8–10 minutes until just softened. Cut in half and scoop out the flesh, reserving the shells.

Heat the oil in a preheated wok or large skillet, add the shallots, garlic, and chilies and stir-fry for 2–3 minutes. Add the zucchini, eggplant flesh, coconut, herbs, and soy sauce and let simmer, stirring frequently, for 3–4 minutes.

Divide the mixture between the eggplant shells. Return to the oven for 5–10 minutes until heated through and serve immediately, accompanied by rice with scallions and sweet chili sauce.

COOK'S TIP
If you can only find large eggplants, one half per person will probably be enough.

serves 4 | prep 15 mins | cook 1¼ – 2¼ hrs

middle eastern baked eggplants

INGREDIENTS

1¼ cups olive oil
1 lb/450 g onions, thinly sliced
6 garlic cloves, thinly sliced
14 oz/400 g canned chopped tomatoes
pinch of sugar
1 tsp salt
2 tbsp chopped fresh parsley
2 tbsp chopped fresh basil
2 eggplants
juice of 1 lemon
lemon wedges, to garnish

Preheat the oven to 325°F/160°C. Heat 4 tablespoons of the oil in a large skillet over high heat. Add the onions and garlic, then reduce the heat to medium–low and cook, stirring frequently, until softened but not browned. Add the tomatoes and bring to a boil, then reduce the heat and let simmer for 5 minutes. Add the sugar, salt, and herbs.

Cut the eggplants in half lengthwise. Put in a large ovenproof dish, cut-side up. Spoon the onion and tomato mixture over the top. Sprinkle with lemon juice and pour over the remaining oil. Add enough water just to cover the topping, then cover the dish and bake in the preheated oven for 1–2 hours until soft. Check frequently during the cooking time, pressing down or adding more water, if necessary.

Remove from the oven, but leave in the dish to cool. To serve, transfer to a serving dish and serve warm or at room temperature, garnished with lemon wedges.

serves 4 | prep 5 mins | cook 1 hr 5 mins

greek beans

INGREDIENTS

**14 oz/400 g canned cannellini
 beans, drained and rinsed**
1 tbsp olive oil
3 garlic cloves, crushed
scant 2 cups vegetable stock
1 bay leaf
2 fresh oregano sprigs
1 tbsp tomato paste
juice of 1 lemon
1 small red onion, chopped
generous ⅛ cup pitted black olives, halved
salt and pepper

Put the beans in an ovenproof casserole over low heat, add the oil and garlic, and cook, stirring frequently, for 4–5 minutes.

Add the stock, bay leaf, oregano, tomato paste, lemon juice, and onion and stir well to mix. Cover and let simmer for 1 hour, or until the sauce has thickened.

Stir in the olives, then season to taste with salt and pepper. This dish is delicious served either warm or cold.

COOK'S TIP
You can substitute other canned beans for the cannellini beans—try kidney or black-eye peas, or chickpeas. Drain and rinse them before use, because canned beans often have sugar or salt added.

serves 6 | prep 15 mins | cook 1 hr 50 mins

frijoles

INGREDIENTS

2 fresh green chilies

2 cups dried red kidney beans, soaked in
cold water for 3 hours

2 onions, chopped

2 garlic cloves, chopped

1 bay leaf

2 tbsp sunflower-seed or corn oil

2 tomatoes, peeled, seeded, and chopped

salt

Chop the chilies. Drain the beans and put in a pan. Add enough water to cover by 1 inch/2.5 cm, half the chopped onion, half the garlic, the chilies, and bay leaf. Bring to a boil and boil vigorously for 15 minutes, then reduce the heat and let simmer for 30 minutes, adding more boiling water if the mixture begins to dry out.

Add half the oil and let simmer for an additional 30 minutes, adding more boiling water, if necessary. Season to taste with salt and let simmer for an additional 30 minutes, but do not add any more water.

Meanwhile, heat the remaining oil in a skillet. Add the remaining onion and garlic and cook, stirring frequently, for 5 minutes, or until softened. Stir in the tomatoes and cook for an additional 5 minutes. Add 3 tablespoons of the cooked beans to the tomato mixture, mash thoroughly into a paste, then stir the paste into the remaining beans. Heat through gently, then serve.

COOK'S TIP

Some dried pulses,
including red kidney beans,
contain a toxin that is
destroyed only by rapid
cooking. It is essential to
boil the beans vigorously
for 15 minutes, before
simmering to finish cooking.

vegetable fajitas

INGREDIENTS
2 tbsp corn oil
2 onions, thinly sliced
2 garlic cloves, finely chopped
2 green bell peppers, seeded and sliced
2 red bell peppers, seeded and sliced
4 fresh green chilies, seeded and sliced
2 tsp chopped fresh cilantro
12 wheat tortillas
8 oz/225 g mushrooms, sliced
salt and pepper

Heat the oil in a heavy-bottom skillet over low heat. Add the onions and garlic and cook, stirring occasionally, for 5 minutes, or until softened. Stir in the bell peppers, chilies, and cilantro and cook, stirring occasionally, for 10 minutes.

Meanwhile, heat a separate, dry skillet over medium–high heat, add a tortilla, and heat for 30 seconds on each side. Remove from the skillet and keep warm in a low oven while you heat the remaining tortillas. Alternatively, put the tortillas in a stack and heat in a microwave oven according to the package instructions.

Add the mushrooms to the vegetable mixture and cook, stirring constantly, for 1 minute. Season to taste with salt and pepper. Divide the vegetables between the tortillas, roll up, and serve immediately.

VARIATION
If you don't like dishes too spicy, use 2 fresh chilies instead of 4, or omit them altogether. The fajitas are good served with plain yogurt or sour cream.

COOK'S TIP
Always wash your hands thoroughly after handling chilies and avoid touching your lips or eyes. If you have sensitive skin, wear rubber gloves.

serves 2–3 | prep 15 mins | cook 1 hr

stuffed bell peppers

INGREDIENTS
6 tbsp olive oil, plus a little extra for rubbing
2 onions, finely chopped
2 garlic cloves, crushed
⅔ cup Spanish short-grain rice
generous ⅓ cup raisins
⅜ cup pine nuts
1½ oz/40 g fresh parsley, finely chopped
1 tbsp tomato paste dissolved in 3 cups
**   hot water**
4–6 red, green, or yellow bell peppers, or a mix of
**   colors, or 6 of the long, Mediterranean variety**
salt and pepper

Heat the oil in a shallow, heavy-bottom, ovenproof casserole over medium heat. Add the onions and cook, stirring, for 3 minutes. Add the garlic and cook, stirring, for an additional 2 minutes, or until the onion is softened but not browned.

Add the rice, raisins, and pine nuts and stir until well coated in the oil. Add half the parsley and salt and pepper to taste, then stir in the dissolved tomato paste and bring to a boil. Reduce the heat and let simmer, uncovered, shaking the casserole frequently, for 20 minutes, or until the rice is tender, the liquid is absorbed and small holes appear on the surface—watch carefully because the raisins can catch and burn easily. Stir in the remaining parsley, then set aside and let cool slightly.

Meanwhile, preheat the oven to 400°F/200°C. Cut the top off each bell pepper and set aside. Remove and discard the core and seeds from each bell pepper.

Divide the stuffing equally between the bell peppers. Use wooden toothpicks to secure the tops back in place. Lightly rub each bell pepper with oil and arrange in a single layer in a baking dish. Bake in the preheated oven for 30 minutes, or until the bell peppers are tender. Serve hot or let cool to room temperature.

COOK'S TIP
If you are using the pointed, Mediterranean variety of pepper, a melon baller, teaspoon or small paring knife makes it easier to remove all the seeds.

serves 4 | prep 20 mins | cook 35–40 mins

stuffed mushrooms

INGREDIENTS
12 large mushrooms
3 tbsp dry white wine
3 tbsp water
1 shallot, chopped
1 fresh thyme sprig, finely chopped
2 tsp lemon juice
1 tbsp butter
2 tsp olive oil
1 garlic clove, finely chopped
3¾ cups fresh spinach leaves, tough stalks removed, chopped
2 oz/55 g feta cheese, crumbled
salt and pepper

Preheat the oven to 350°F/180°C. Remove and finely chop the mushroom stalks.

Pour the wine and water into a wide pan and add half the shallot and the thyme. Bring to a boil over medium heat, then reduce the heat and let simmer for 2 minutes. Add the mushroom caps, smooth-side down, and sprinkle over the lemon juice. Cover and let simmer for 6 minutes, then remove the mushrooms and place on a plate to drain. Return the liquid to a boil, add the mushroom stalks and butter, and season to taste with salt. Cook for 6 minutes, or until the liquid has been absorbed. Transfer the stalks to a bowl.

Heat the oil in a clean pan over medium heat. Add the remaining shallot, garlic, and spinach and sprinkle with a little salt. Cook, stirring, for 3 minutes, or until all the liquid has evaporated. Stir the spinach mixture into the mushroom stalks,

season to taste with pepper, then gently stir in the feta cheese.

Divide the spinach mixture evenly between the mushroom caps. Put in a single layer in an ovenproof dish and bake in the preheated oven for 15–20 minutes until golden. Serve warm.

serves 4 | prep 10 mins | cook 1 hr 10 mins

stuffed baked potatoes

INGREDIENTS
2 lb/900 g baking potatoes, scrubbed
2 tbsp vegetable oil
1 tsp coarse sea salt
½ cup butter
1 small onion, chopped
1 cup grated Cheddar cheese or crumbled
  blue cheese
salt and pepper

OPTIONAL
4 tbsp canned, drained corn kernels
4 tbsp cooked mushrooms, zucchini, or peppers

snipped fresh chives, to garnish

Preheat the oven to 375°F/190°C. Prick the potatoes in several places with a fork and put on a baking sheet. Brush with the oil and sprinkle with the salt. Bake in the preheated oven for 1 hour, or until the skins are crispy and the insides are soft when pierced with a fork.

Meanwhile, melt 1 tablespoon of the butter in a small skillet over medium–low heat. Add the onion and cook, stirring occasionally, for 8–10 minutes until soft and golden. Set aside.

Cut the potatoes in half lengthwise. Scoop the flesh into a large bowl, leaving the skins intact. Set aside the skins. Increase the oven temperature to 400°F/200°C.

Coarsely mash the potato flesh and mix in the onion and remaining butter. Add salt and pepper to taste and stir in any of the optional ingredients. Spoon the mixture back into the reserved potato skins. Top with the cheese.

Cook the filled potato skins in the oven for 10 minutes, or until the cheese has melted and is beginning to brown. Garnish with chives and serve immediately.

serves 4 | prep 20 mins | cook 1 hr 10 mins

potato skins
with tomato & corn salsa

INGREDIENTS
2 large baking potatoes
3 oz/85 g canned corn kernels
2 oz/55 g canned kidney beans
2 tbsp olive oil, plus extra for brushing
4 oz/115 g tomatoes, seeded and diced
2 shallots, finely sliced
¼ red bell pepper, finely diced
1 fresh red chili, seeded and finely chopped
1 tbsp chopped fresh cilantro leaves
1 tbsp lime juice
2 oz/55 g Cheddar cheese, grated
salt and pepper
lime wedges, to garnish

Preheat the oven to 400°F/200°C. Prick the potatoes in several places with a fork and brush with oil. Cook directly on the oven shelf for 1 hour, or until the skins are crispy and the insides are soft when pierced with a fork.

Meanwhile, make the salsa. Drain the corn and beans, rinse well, then drain again. Put in a bowl with the oil, tomatoes, shallots, red bell pepper, chili, cilantro, lime juice, and salt and pepper to taste and mix well together.

Preheat the broiler to medium. Cut the potatoes in half lengthwise. Scoop out the flesh (set aside for use in another recipe), leaving the skins intact. Brush the insides with oil, then put on a baking sheet, cut-sides up. Cook under the broiler for 5 minutes, or until crisp.

Spoon the salsa into the potato skins and sprinkle the cheese over the top. Return the filled potato skins to the broiler and cook gently until the cheese has melted. Serve immediately, garnished with lime wedges.

serves 4 | prep 15 mins | cook 20 mins

bean burgers

INGREDIENTS

1 tbsp sunflower-seed oil, plus extra for brushing
1 onion, finely chopped
1 garlic clove, finely chopped
1 tsp ground coriander
1 tsp ground cumin
4 oz/115 g white mushrooms, finely chopped
15 oz/425 g canned pinto or red kidney beans,
  drained and rinsed
2 tbsp chopped fresh flat-leaf parsley
all-purpose flour, for dusting
salt and pepper

TO SERVE
hamburger buns
salad

Heat the oil in a heavy-bottom skillet over medium heat. Add the onion and cook, stirring frequently, for 5 minutes, or until softened. Add the garlic, coriander, and cumin and cook, stirring, for an additional minute. Add the mushrooms and cook, stirring frequently, for 4–5 minutes until all the liquid has evaporated. Transfer to a bowl.

Put the beans in a small bowl and mash with a fork. Stir into the mushroom mixture with the parsley and season to taste with salt and pepper.

Preheat the broiler to medium–high. Divide the mixture equally into 4 portions, dust lightly with flour, and shape into flat, round patties. Brush with oil and cook under the broiler for 4–5 minutes on each side. Serve in hamburger buns with salad.

COOK'S TIP
If the burgers do not hold together when you try to shape them, add just a little more oil to the mixture to make them easier to handle.

serves 4 | prep 15 mins | cook 15 mins

cauliflower cheese

INGREDIENTS
**1 cauliflower, cut into florets, about
  1 lb 8 oz/675 g prepared weight
3 tbsp butter
scant ⅓ cup all-purpose flour
2 cups milk
4 oz/115 g Cheddar cheese, finely grated
whole nutmeg, for grating
1 tbsp freshly grated Parmesan cheese
salt and pepper**

TO SERVE
**sliced tomatoes
green salad
crusty bread**

Bring a large pan of salted water to a boil, add the cauliflower, and cook for 4–5 minutes—it should still be firm. Drain, place in a hot 6-cup gratin dish and keep warm.

Melt the butter in the rinsed-out pan over medium heat and stir in the flour. Cook for 1 minute, stirring constantly.

Remove from the heat and gradually stir in the milk until smooth.

Return to medium heat and cook, stirring constantly, until the sauce comes to a boil and thickens. Reduce the heat to low and let simmer gently, stirring constantly, for 3 minutes, or until the sauce is creamy and smooth.

Remove from the heat and stir in the Cheddar cheese and a generous grating of the nutmeg. Taste and season well with salt and pepper.

Preheat the broiler to high. Pour the hot sauce over the cauliflower, top with the Parmesan cheese, and cook under the broiler until browned. Serve immediately, accompanied by sliced tomatoes, green salad, and crusty bread.

serves 4 | prep 10 mins | cook 15 mins

cheesy baked zucchini

INGREDIENTS

4 zucchini

2 tbsp extra virgin olive oil

4 oz/115 g mozzarella cheese, thinly sliced

2 large tomatoes, seeded and diced

**2 tsp fresh basil or oregano, chopped, plus extra
leaves to garnish**

Preheat the oven to 400°F/200°C. Slice the zucchini lengthwise into 4 strips each. Brush with oil and put in an ovenproof dish.

Bake the zucchini in the preheated oven for 10 minutes, or until softened but still holding their shape.

Remove from the oven. Arrange the cheese slices on top and sprinkle with the tomatoes and basil. Return to the oven for 5 minutes, or until the cheese has melted.

Carefully transfer the zucchini to serving plates, or serve straight from the baking dish, garnished with basil leaves.

serves 4 | prep 15 mins | cook 5–7 mins

classic stir-fried vegetables

INGREDIENTS

3 tbsp sesame oil
8 scallions, finely chopped
1 garlic clove, crushed
1 tbsp grated fresh gingerroot
1 head of broccoli, cut into florets
1 orange or yellow bell pepper, coarsely chopped
4½ oz/125 g red cabbage, shredded
4½ oz/125 g baby corn
6 oz/175 g portobello or large cup mushrooms,
  thinly sliced
1⅓ cups fresh bean sprouts
250 g/9 oz canned water chestnuts,
  drained and rinsed
4 tsp soy sauce, or to taste
cooked mixed long-grain and wild rice, to serve

Heat 2 tablespoons of the oil in a preheated wok or large skillet over high heat. Add 6 of the scallions, the garlic and ginger and stir-fry for 30 seconds. Reserve the remaining scallions for garnishing.

Add the broccoli, orange bell pepper, and cabbage and stir-fry for 1–2 minutes. Add the corn and mushrooms and stir-fry for an additional 1–2 minutes.

Finally, add the bean sprouts and water chestnuts and stir-fry for an additional 2 minutes. Add the soy sauce and stir well.

Transfer to warmed dishes and serve immediately over cooked mixed long-grain and wild rice, garnished with the reserved scallions.

serves 4–6 | prep 10 mins, plus 15 mins' standing | cook 15–30 mins

spanish tortilla

INGREDIENTS
½ cup olive oil
1 lb 5 oz/600 g potatoes, peeled and thinly sliced
1 large onion, thinly sliced
6 large eggs
salt and pepper
fresh flat-leaf parsley sprigs, to garnish

Heat a 10-inch/25-cm skillet, preferably nonstick, over high heat. Add the oil and heat. Reduce the heat to medium–low, then add the potatoes and onion and cook, stirring occasionally, for 15–20 minutes until the potatoes are tender.

Beat the eggs in a large bowl and season generously with salt and pepper. Very gently stir the vegetables into the eggs. Set aside for 10 minutes. Drain the potatoes and onion through a strainer over a heatproof bowl to reserve the oil.

Use a wooden spoon or spatula to remove any crusty bits stuck to the bottom of the skillet. Reheat the skillet over medium–high heat with 4 tablespoons of the reserved oil. Add the egg mixture and level the surface, pressing the potatoes and onions into an even layer.

Cook, shaking the pan occasionally, for 5 minutes, or until the bottom is set. Use a spatula to loosen the side of the tortilla. Put a large plate over the top and carefully invert the skillet and plate together so that the tortilla drops onto the plate. Add 1 tablespoon of the remaining reserved oil to the skillet and swirl around. Carefully slide the tortilla back into the pan, cooked-side up. Run the spatula around the tortilla, to tuck in the edge.

Cook for an additional 3 minutes, or until the eggs are set and the bottom is golden brown. Remove from the heat and slide the tortilla onto a plate. Let stand for at least 5 minutes before cutting. Serve warm or at room temperature, garnished with parsley sprigs.

COOK'S TIP
If you are uncomfortable about inverting the tortilla, finish cooking it under a medium–high broiler, about 4 inches/10 cm from the heat source, until the runny egg mixture on top is set. The tortilla will not, however, have its characteristic "rounded" edge.

serves 4 | prep 15 mins | cook 15 mins

glazed vegetable kabobs

INGREDIENTS
⅔ cup lowfat plain yogurt
4 tbsp mango chutney
1 tsp chopped garlic
1 tbsp lemon juice
8 pearl onions, peeled but left whole
16 baby corn, halved
2 zucchini, cut into 1-inch/2.5-cm pieces
16 white mushrooms
16 cherry tomatoes
salt and pepper
mixed salad greens, to garnish

Put the yogurt, chutney, garlic, lemon juice, and salt and pepper to taste in a bowl, stir together and set aside.

Bring a pan of water to a boil, add the onions, and return to a boil. Remove from the heat and drain well.

Thread the onions, corn, zucchini, mushrooms, and tomatoes alternately onto 8 metal skewers or bamboo skewers presoaked in water for 30 minutes.

Preheat the broiler to high. Arrange the kabobs on a broiler rack and brush with the yogurt mixture. Cook under the broiler, turning and brushing frequently with the remaining yogurt mixture, for 10 minutes, or until golden and tender.

Serve garnished with mixed salad greens.

serves 4 | prep 15 mins | cook 20 mins

warm vegetable medley

INGREDIENTS
4 tbsp olive oil
2 celery stalks, sliced
2 red onions, sliced
1 lb/450 g eggplants, diced
1 garlic clove, finely chopped
5 plum tomatoes, chopped
3 tbsp red wine vinegar
1 tbsp sugar
3 tbsp green olives, pitted
2 tbsp capers
4 tbsp chopped fresh flat-leaf parsley
salt and pepper
hunks of fresh bread or rolls, to serve

Heat half the oil in a large, heavy-bottom pan over low heat. Add the celery and onions and cook, stirring frequently, for 5 minutes, or until softened but not browned. Add the remaining oil and the eggplants and cook, stirring frequently, for 5 minutes, or until the eggplants start to brown.

Add the garlic, tomatoes, vinegar, and sugar and mix well. Cover the mixture with a circle of waxed paper and let simmer gently for 10 minutes.

Remove and discard the waxed paper, stir in the olives and capers and season to taste with salt and pepper. Tip the mixture into a serving dish and set aside to cool to room temperature. Sprinkle over the parsley and serve with hunks of bread or rolls.

COOK'S TIP
If possible, buy Sicilian capers for this dish. They are packed in salt and just need rinsing before use. Otherwise, use capers pickled in brine, but avoid those that are bottled in vinegar.

serves 4 | prep 15 mins | cook 5–8 mins

sweet-&-sour vegetables with cashews

INGREDIENTS
1 tbsp vegetable or peanut oil
1 tsp chili oil
2 onions, sliced
2 carrots, thinly sliced
2 zucchini, thinly sliced
4 oz/115 g broccoli, cut into florets
4 oz/115 g white mushrooms, sliced
4 oz/115 g small bok choy, halved
2 tbsp jaggery or brown sugar
2 tbsp Thai soy sauce
1 tbsp rice vinegar
generous ⅓ cup cashews

Heat both the oils in a preheated wok or skillet, add the onions, and stir-fry for 1–2 minutes until beginning to soften.

Add the carrots, zucchini, and broccoli and stir-fry for 2–3 minutes. Add the mushrooms, bok choy, sugar, soy sauce, and vinegar and stir-fry for 1–2 minutes.

Meanwhile, heat a dry, heavy-bottom skillet over high heat, add the cashews, and cook, shaking the skillet frequently, until lightly toasted. Sprinkle the cashews over the stir-fry and serve immediately.

serves 4 | prep 10 mins, plus 20 mins' marinating | cook 10 mins

spicy tofu

INGREDIENTS

MARINADE
5 tbsp vegetable stock
2 tsp cornstarch
2 tbsp soy sauce
1 tbsp superfine sugar
pinch of dried red pepper flakes

STIR-FRY
9 oz/250 g firm tofu (drained weight),
  rinsed and drained thoroughly, then cut into
  ½-inch/1-cm cubes
4 tbsp peanut oil
1 tbsp grated fresh gingerroot
3 garlic cloves, crushed
4 scallions, thinly sliced
1 head of broccoli, cut into florets
1 carrot, cut into thin sticks
1 yellow bell pepper, thinly sliced
9 oz/250 g shiitake mushrooms, thinly sliced
steamed rice, to serve

Blend all the marinade ingredients together in a large bowl. Add the tofu and toss well to coat. Cover and set aside to marinate for 20 minutes.

Heat half the oil in a preheated wok or large skillet over high heat, add the tofu with its marinade, and stir-fry until browned and crisp. Remove from the wok and set aside.

Heat the remaining oil in the wok, add the ginger, garlic, and scallions and stir-fry for 30 seconds.

Add the broccoli, carrot, yellow bell pepper, and mushrooms and stir-fry for 5–6 minutes. Return the tofu to the wok and stir-fry to heat through.

Serve at once with steamed rice.

serves 4 | prep 10 mins | cook 6 mins

oyster mushrooms & vegetables with peanut chili sauce

INGREDIENTS
1 tbsp sesame oil
4 scallions, finely sliced
1 carrot, cut into thin sticks
1 zucchini, cut into thin sticks
½ head of broccoli, cut into florets
1 lb/450 g oyster mushrooms, thinly sliced
2 tbsp crunchy peanut butter
1 tsp chili powder, or to taste
3 tbsp water
lime wedges, to garnish
cooked rice or noodles, to serve

Heat the oil in a preheated wok or large skillet until almost smoking, add the scallions and stir-fry for 1 minute. Add the carrot and zucchini and stir-fry for 1 minute. Add the broccoli and stir-fry for an additional minute.

Add the mushrooms and stir-fry until softened and at least half the liquid they have produced has evaporated. Add the peanut butter and stir well, then add the chili powder.

Finally, add the water and cook, stirring, for an additional minute. Serve at once over cooked rice or noodles, garnished with lime wedges.

4

The following selection of main-course recipes shows just how varied vegetarian food can be. Here you will find definitive vegetarian versions of those perennially popular dishes—lasagna, moussaka, chili, and paella—along with that other crowd-pleasing standard, the nut loaf, featuring hazelnuts, carrots, and cilantro.

MAIN MEALS

Pasta fans are further catered for with a range of fresh vegetable and herb sauces, while rice lovers can feast on mouthwatering variations on the classic risotto theme. And curry enthusiasts have the pick of Thai- or Indian-style dishes, according to individual preference or mood. But for universal appeal and everyday satisfaction, a heartwarming stew is the easy winner.

serves 4 | prep 10 mins, plus 30 mins' standing | cook 45 mins

ratatouille with baked jacket potatoes

INGREDIENTS

1 eggplant, about 9 oz/250 g
4 tbsp olive oil
2 garlic cloves, chopped
1 large onion, chopped
2 red bell peppers, seeded and cut into
** bite-size chunks**
1 lb 12 oz/800 g canned chopped tomatoes
2 zucchini, sliced
1 celery stalk, sliced
1 tsp sugar
salt and pepper
2 tbsp chopped fresh thyme, plus extra sprigs
** to garnish**

TO SERVE

freshly baked jacket potatoes with butter
fresh crusty bread

Trim the eggplant, cut it into bite-size chunks, and put in a colander. Sprinkle with salt and let stand for about 30 minutes.

Heat the oil in a large pan over medium heat. Add the garlic and onion and cook, stirring frequently, for 3 minutes, or until slightly softened. Rinse the eggplant and drain well, then add it to the pan with the bell peppers. Reduce the heat and cook gently, stirring occasionally, for an additional 10 minutes.

Stir in the tomatoes, zucchini, celery, sugar, and chopped thyme and season to taste with salt and pepper. Bring to a boil, then reduce the heat, cover, and let simmer gently for 30 minutes.

Remove from the heat, transfer to serving plates, and garnish with thyme sprigs. Serve with buttered hot jacket potatoes and crusty bread.

serves 4 | prep 10 mins, plus 30 mins' standing | cook 1¼ hrs

imam bayildi

INGREDIENTS
2 eggplants, about 9¾ oz/275 g each
6 tbsp olive oil
3 garlic cloves, chopped
2 onions, chopped
1 lb 10 oz/750 g canned chopped tomatoes
2 red bell peppers, seeded and chopped
1 celery stalk, sliced
1 tbsp raisins
1 tbsp golden raisins
pinch of freshly grated nutmeg
salt and pepper
1 tbsp chopped fresh flat-leaf parsley, plus extra
** sprigs to garnish**
freshly cooked rice, to serve

Cut each eggplant in half lengthwise. Scoop out the flesh, leaving ½ inch/1 cm of flesh around the inside of each shell. Chop the flesh. Sprinkle the flesh and shells with salt and let stand for 30 minutes.

Preheat the oven to 350°F/180°C. Heat half the oil in a pan over medium heat. Add the garlic and onion and cook, stirring frequently, for 3 minutes, or until slightly softened. Rinse the eggplant and drain well, then add the flesh to the pan with the tomatoes, reserving the shells. Cook, stirring frequently, for 10 minutes. Add the red bell peppers, celery, raisins, golden raisins, nutmeg, and chopped parsley to the pan and season to taste with salt and pepper. Reduce the heat, cover, and let simmer for 15 minutes.

Put the eggplant shells in an ovenproof dish. Spoon the tomato mixture into the shells. Drizzle with the remaining oil, cover with foil, and bake in the preheated oven for 45 minutes. Remove from the oven and let cool to room temperature. Garnish with parsley sprigs and serve with freshly cooked rice. Alternatively, to serve cold, let the eggplants cool completely, cover with plastic wrap, and chill in the refrigerator until required. Remove from the refrigerator 1 hour before serving.

cannelloni with spinach & ricotta

INGREDIENTS
12 dried cannelloni tubes, 3 inches/7.5 cm long
butter, for greasing

FILLING
¾ cup frozen spinach, thawed and drained
½ cup ricotta cheese
1 egg
3 tbsp freshly grated romano cheese
pinch of freshly grated nutmeg
salt and pepper

CHEESE SAUCE
2½ cups milk
2 tbsp unsalted butter
2 tbsp all-purpose flour
¾ cup freshly grated Gruyère cheese
salt and pepper

Bring a large pan of lightly salted water to a boil. Add the cannelloni tubes, return to a boil, and cook for 6–7 minutes until almost tender. Drain, refresh under cold running water, and drain again. Spread out the tubes on a clean dish towel.

Put the spinach and ricotta in a blender or food processor and process for a few seconds until combined. Add the egg and romano cheese and process again to a smooth paste. Scrape the filling into a bowl and season to taste with nutmeg and salt and pepper.

Preheat the oven to 350°F/180°C. Grease an ovenproof dish. Spoon the filling into a pastry bag fitted with a ½-inch/1-cm tip. Pipe the filling into a cannelloni tube. Put the filled cannelloni tube in the prepared dish, then fill the remaining cannelloni tubes with the mixture.

To make the cheese sauce, heat the milk in a pan to just below boiling point. Meanwhile, melt the butter in a separate pan over low heat. Add the flour to the butter and cook, stirring constantly, for 1 minute. Remove from the heat and gradually stir in the hot milk. Return to the heat and bring to a boil, stirring constantly. Reduce the heat to the lowest possible setting and let simmer, stirring frequently, for 10 minutes, or until thickened and smooth. Remove from the heat, stir in the Gruyère cheese, and season to taste with salt and pepper.

Spoon the cheese sauce over the filled cannelloni. Cover the dish with foil and bake in the preheated oven for 20–25 minutes. Serve immediately.

serves 4 | prep 10 mins | cook 25 mins

fusilli with zucchini, lemon & rosemary sauce

INGREDIENTS

6 tbsp olive oil
1 small onion, very thinly sliced
2 garlic cloves, very finely chopped
2 tbsp chopped fresh rosemary
1 tbsp chopped fresh flat-leaf parsley
1 lb/450 g small zucchini, cut into
  1½-x-¼-inch/4-cm-x-5-mm strips
finely grated rind of 1 lemon
1 lb/450 g dried fusilli
4 tbsp freshly grated Parmesan cheese
salt and pepper

Heat the oil in a large skillet over medium–low heat. Add the onion and cook, stirring occasionally, for 10 minutes, or until golden.

Increase the heat to medium–high. Add the garlic, rosemary, and parsley and cook, stirring, for a few seconds.

Add the zucchini and lemon rind and cook, stirring occasionally, for 5–7 minutes until the zucchini are just tender. Season to taste with salt and pepper. Remove from the heat.

Meanwhile, bring a large pan of salted water to a boil. Add the pasta, return to a boil, and cook for 8–10 minutes until tender but still firm to the bite. Drain the pasta and transfer to a warmed serving dish.

Briefly reheat the zucchini sauce. Pour over the pasta and toss well to mix. Sprinkle with the Parmesan cheese and serve immediately.

pasta all'arrabbiata

INGREDIENTS
⅔ **cup dry white wine**
1 tbsp sun-dried tomato paste
2 fresh red chilies
2 garlic cloves, finely chopped
12 oz/350 g dried tortiglioni
4 tbsp chopped fresh flat-leaf parsley
salt and pepper
fresh romano cheese shavings, to garnish

SUGOCASA
5 tbsp extra virgin olive oil
1 lb/450 g plum tomatoes, chopped
salt and pepper

First make the sugocasa. Heat the oil in a skillet over high heat until almost smoking. Add the tomatoes and cook, stirring frequently, for 2–3 minutes. Reduce the heat to low and cook gently for 20 minutes, or until very soft. Season to taste with salt and pepper. Press through a nonmetallic strainer with a wooden spoon into a pan.

Add the wine, tomato paste, whole chilies, and garlic to the sugocasa and bring to a boil. Reduce the heat and let simmer gently.

Meanwhile, bring a large pan of lightly salted water to a boil. Add the pasta, return to a boil, and cook for 8–10 minutes until tender but still firm to the bite.

Remove the chilies and taste the sauce. If you prefer a hotter flavor, chop some or all of the chilies and return to the pan. Check and adjust the seasoning, if necessary, then stir in half the parsley.

Drain the pasta and transfer to a warmed serving bowl. Add the sauce and toss to coat. Sprinkle with the remaining parsley, garnish with the romano cheese shavings, and serve immediately.

COOK'S TIP
If time is short, use ready-made sugocasa, available from most supermarkets and sometimes labeled "crushed tomatoes." You can also use strained canned tomatoes, but the sauce will be thinner.

serves 4 | prep 10 mins | cook 20 mins

chili broccoli pasta

INGREDIENTS

8 oz/225 g dried penne or macaroni
8 oz/225 g broccoli, cut into florets
¼ cup extra virgin olive oil
2 large garlic cloves, chopped
2 fresh red chilies, seeded and diced
8 cherry tomatoes (optional)
fresh basil leaves, to garnish

Bring a large pan of salted boiling water to a boil. Add the pasta, return to a boil, and cook for 8–10 minutes until tender but still firm to the bite. Drain the pasta, refresh under cold running water, and drain again. Set aside.

Bring a separate pan of salted water to a boil, add the broccoli, and cook for 5 minutes. Drain, refresh under cold running water, and drain again.

Heat the oil in the pan that the pasta was cooked in over high heat. Add the garlic, chilies, and tomatoes, if using, and cook, stirring, for 1 minute.

Add the broccoli and mix well. Cook for 2 minutes, stirring, to heat through. Add the pasta and mix well again. Cook for an additional minute. Transfer the pasta to a large, warmed serving bowl and serve garnished with basil leaves.

serves 4 | prep 10 mins, plus 30 mins' standing | cook 8–10 mins

conchiglie with raw tomato, garlic & basil sauce

INGREDIENTS

1 lb 4 oz/550 g large, ripe tomatoes, peeled, seeded, and diced
½ cup extra virgin olive oil
4 garlic cloves, very finely chopped
large handful of fresh basil leaves, shredded
3 tbsp chopped fresh oregano or marjoram
1 lb/450 g dried conchiglie
salt and pepper

Combine the tomatoes, oil, garlic, basil, and oregano in a bowl that is large enough to accommodate the cooked pasta. Season generously with salt and pepper. Cover the bowl with plastic wrap and let stand at room temperature for at least 30 minutes.

Bring a large pan of salted water to a boil. Add the pasta, return to a boil, and cook for 8–10 minutes until tender but still firm to the bite. Drain thoroughly and add immediately to the tomato mixture.

Toss well to mix. Serve at room temperature.

serves 4 | prep 5 mins | cook 30 mins

basic risotto

INGREDIENTS
8½ cups vegetable stock or water
3 tbsp butter
1 tbsp olive oil
1 small onion, finely chopped
1 lb/450 g risotto rice
salt and pepper
½ cup freshly grated Parmesan or
Grana Padano cheese, plus extra shavings
to garnish

Bring the stock to a boil in a pan, then reduce the heat and keep simmering gently over low heat while you are cooking the risotto.

Melt 2 tablespoons of the butter with the oil in a deep pan over medium heat. Add the onion and cook, stirring frequently, for 5 minutes, or until softened but not browned.

Add the rice, stir to coat in the butter and oil, and cook, stirring constantly, for 2–3 minutes until the grains are translucent. Gradually add the hot stock, a ladle at a time, stirring constantly and adding more liquid as the rice absorbs it. Cook for 20 minutes, or until all the liquid is absorbed and the risotto is creamy but there is still a little bite to the rice. Season to taste with salt and pepper, but bear in mind that the Parmesan cheese is salty.

Remove from the heat and add the remaining butter. Mix well, then stir in the Parmesan cheese until it has melted. Taste and adjust the seasoning, if necessary, and serve immediately, garnished with Parmesan cheese shavings.

serves 4 | prep 5 mins | cook 30 mins

red wine, herb & sun-dried tomato risotto

INGREDIENTS

1 quantity basic risotto, made with half vegetable stock, half strong Italian red wine

6 sun-dried tomatoes in olive oil, drained and finely chopped

1 tbsp chopped fresh thyme, plus extra sprigs to garnish

1 tbsp chopped fresh parsley

10–12 fresh basil leaves, shredded, to garnish

Prepare the basic risotto, folding in the sun-dried tomatoes after the first addition of stock-wine mixture has been absorbed.

Carefully fold the herbs into the risotto 5 minutes before the end of cooking time.

Serve the risotto garnished with the shredded basil leaves and thyme sprigs.

serves 4 | prep 5 mins | cook 30 mins

risotto with roasted vegetables

INGREDIENTS

**1 quantity basic risotto, made with vegetable
stock or half stock and half dry white wine
8 oz/225 g roasted vegetables, such as bell
peppers, zucchini, and eggplant, cut into chunks
2 tbsp fresh herbs, finely chopped, to garnish**

Prepare the basic risotto, adding most of the
roasted vegetables to the risotto 5 minutes before
the end of cooking time to heat through. Set aside
a few large pieces for garnishing.

Spoon the risotto onto individual warmed plates,
arrange the reserved vegetables around it or on
top to garnish, then sprinkle with fresh herbs
before serving immediately.

vegetable paella

INGREDIENTS
¼ tsp saffron threads
3 tbsp hot water
6 tbsp olive oil
1 Spanish onion, sliced
3 garlic cloves, finely chopped
1 red bell pepper, seeded and sliced
1 orange bell pepper, seeded and sliced
1 large eggplant, cut into cubes
generous 1 cup risotto rice
2½ cups vegetable stock
1 lb/450 g tomatoes, peeled and chopped
4 oz/115 g mushrooms, sliced
4 oz/115 g green beans, halved
14 oz/400 g canned pinto beans
salt and pepper

Put the saffron and water in a bowl and set aside. Meanwhile, heat the oil in a large skillet or paella pan over medium heat. Add the onion and cook, stirring frequently, for 5 minutes, or until softened. Add the garlic, bell peppers, and eggplant and cook, stirring occasionally, for 5 minutes.

Add the rice and cook, stirring constantly, for 1 minute, or until the grains are well coated in oil.

Stir in the stock, tomatoes, and saffron and its soaking liquid and season to taste with salt and pepper. Bring to a boil, then reduce the heat and let simmer, shaking the skillet frequently and stirring occasionally, for 15 minutes.

Stir in the mushrooms, green beans, and pinto beans with their juices. Cook for an additional 10 minutes. Serve immediately.

serves 4 | prep 30 mins | cook 15 mins

lentil & rice pilaf
with celery, carrots & orange

INGREDIENTS
4 tbsp vegetable oil
1 red onion, finely chopped
2 tender celery stalks, leaves included,
 quartered lengthwise and diced
2 carrots, coarsely grated
1 fresh green chili, seeded and finely chopped
3 scallions, green parts included, finely
 chopped
generous ¼ cup whole blanched almonds,
 sliced lengthwise
1¾ cups cooked brown basmati rice
¾ cup cooked red split lentils
¾ cup vegetable stock
5 tbsp fresh orange juice
salt and pepper

Heat half the oil in a high-sided skillet with a lid over medium heat. Add the onion and cook, stirring frequently, for 5 minutes, or until softened.

Add the celery, carrots, chili, scallions, and almonds. Stir-fry for 2 minutes, or until the vegetables are al dente but still brightly colored. Transfer to a bowl and set aside.

Add the remaining oil to the skillet over medium–high heat. Add the rice and lentils and cook, stirring, for 1–2 minutes until heated through. Reduce the heat and stir in the stock and orange juice. Season to taste with salt and pepper.

Return the vegetables to the skillet. Toss with the rice for a few minutes until heated through. Transfer to a warmed serving dish and serve immediately.

serves 4 | prep 10 mins | cook 1½ hrs

caribbean rice & peas

INGREDIENTS

⅔ cup dried pigeon peas, soaked overnight
  in water to cover
generous 1⅛ cups long-grain rice
3 cups water
1 onion, chopped
2 garlic cloves, finely chopped
1 small red bell pepper, seeded and chopped
1 tbsp fresh thyme leaves
1 bay leaf
½ tsp ground allspice
⅛ cup coconut cream
salt and pepper

COOK'S TIP

*Pigeon peas go by a variety
of names, including gunga,
Congo, and Jamaica peas.
Fresh pigeon peas,
sometimes known as Cajun
peas, also feature in
Caribbean cooking.*

Drain the pigeon peas and put in a large pan. Add enough cold water to cover by about 1 inch/ 2.5 cm. Bring to a boil, then reduce the heat and let simmer for 1 hour, or until tender. Drain and return to the pan.

Add the rice, water, onion, garlic, red bell pepper, thyme, bay leaf, and allspice and season to taste with salt and pepper. Bring to a boil, then reduce the heat, cover, and let simmer for 20 minutes.

Uncover the pan, stir in the coconut cream and cook the rice mixture for an additional 5 minutes, or until any excess liquid has evaporated. Fork through the rice to fluff up the grains, then serve immediately.

serves 4 | prep 15 mins, plus 30 mins' standing | cook 1 hr

vegetable polenta

INGREDIENTS

1 eggplant, about 9 oz/250 g, sliced
scant 2 cups cornmeal
5 cups vegetable stock
6 tbsp olive oil, plus extra for oiling
1 garlic clove, chopped
2 red onions, sliced
1 lb 14 oz/850 g small new potatoes, halved
1 red bell pepper, seeded and cut into strips
1 orange bell pepper, seeded and cut into strips
2 zucchini, sliced
3 tbsp sun-dried tomatoes in olive oil,
  drained and chopped
1 tbsp chopped fresh rosemary
salt and pepper
1 tbsp chopped fresh flat-leaf parsley,
  plus extra sprigs to garnish

Put the eggplant slices in a colander. Sprinkle with salt and let stand for 30 minutes.

Preheat the oven to 375°F/190°C. Oil an ovenproof dish. Put the cornmeal and stock in a large pan and bring to a boil, stirring constantly. Boil for 10 minutes, stirring, then transfer to the oiled dish. Bake in the preheated oven for 45 minutes, turning the cornmeal over halfway through the cooking time.

Meanwhile, heat half the oil in a large pan over medium heat. Add the garlic and onions and cook, stirring frequently, for 3 minutes. Rinse the eggplant, drain well, and pat dry. Add to the pan with the potatoes, bell peppers, zucchini, tomatoes, rosemary, and parsley. Season to taste with salt and pepper. Cook, stirring frequently, for 5 minutes, then reduce the heat and cook, stirring occasionally, for 10 minutes.

Lightly oil a baking sheet and spread the vegetables out on it. Drizzle over the remaining oil, then roast in the oven for 20 minutes, turning over halfway through the cooking time. To serve, cut the cornmeal into wedges and arrange with the roasted vegetables on serving plates, garnished with parsley sprigs.

serves 4 | prep 15 mins | cook 20 mins

thai green curry

INGREDIENTS

5½ oz/150 g broccoli florets

5½ oz/150 g snow peas

2 tbsp chili oil

1½ cups canned coconut milk

7 oz/200 g firm marinated tofu, cut into cubes

1 green bell pepper, seeded and sliced

1 yellow bell pepper, seeded and sliced

1 tbsp soy sauce

⅔ cup bean sprouts

1 tbsp chopped fresh cilantro, plus extra
   sprigs to garnish

salt and pepper

freshly cooked noodles, to serve

GREEN CURRY PASTE

8 fresh green chilies, chopped

2 tbsp chopped scallions

2 tsp chopped fresh kaffir lime leaves

2 large garlic cloves, finely chopped

1-inch/2.5-cm piece fresh gingerroot, grated

1 tbsp finely chopped fresh lemon grass

2 tsp ground coriander

½ tsp ground cumin

½ tsp salt

2 tbsp chili oil

To make the green curry paste, put all the ingredients in a food processor and process until smooth. Transfer to a bowl, cover with plastic wrap, and refrigerate until required. Bring a large pan of water to a boil, add the broccoli and snow peas, and cook for 2 minutes. Drain, refresh under cold running water, then drain again.

Heat the oil in a large pan over medium heat, add 2 tablespoons of the curry paste, and cook, stirring, for 1 minute. Stir in 4 tablespoons of the coconut milk, then add the tofu, broccoli, snow peas, bell peppers, and soy sauce. Cook for 5 minutes, then stir in the remaining coconut milk and bring to a boil. Reduce the heat, add the bean sprouts, and cook for an additional 5 minutes. Stir in the chopped cilantro, season to taste with salt and pepper, and heat through.

Spoon over freshly cooked noodles, garnish with cilantro sprigs, and serve immediately.

serves 4 | prep 20 mins | cook 40–50 mins

vegetable & coconut curry

INGREDIENTS

1 onion, coarsely chopped

3 garlic cloves, thinly sliced

1-inch/2.5-cm piece fresh gingerroot, thinly sliced

2 fresh green chilies, seeded and
  finely chopped

1 tbsp vegetable oil

1 tsp ground turmeric

1 tsp ground coriander

1 tsp ground cumin

2 lb 4 oz/1 kg mixed vegetables, such as
cauliflower, zucchini, potatoes, carrots, and
  green beans, cut into chunks

scant 1 cup coconut cream or milk

salt and pepper

2 tbsp chopped fresh cilantro, to garnish

freshly cooked rice, to serve

Put the onion, garlic, ginger, and chilies in a food processor and process until almost smooth.

Heat the oil in a large, heavy-bottom pan over medium–low heat, add the onion mixture, and cook, stirring constantly, for 5 minutes.

Add the turmeric, ground coriander, and cumin and cook, stirring frequently, for 3–4 minutes. Add the vegetables and stir to coat in the spice paste.

Add the coconut cream or milk to the vegetables, cover, and let simmer for 30–40 minutes until the vegetables are tender.

Season to taste with salt and pepper, garnish with the chopped fresh cilantro, and serve with rice.

serves 4 | prep 20 mins | cook 45 mins

mixed vegetable curry

INGREDIENTS

1 eggplant
8 oz/225 g turnips
12 oz/350 g new potatoes
8 oz/225 g cauliflower
8 oz/225 g white mushrooms
1 large onion
3 carrots
6 tbsp ghee or vegetable oil
2 garlic cloves, crushed
4 tsp finely chopped fresh gingerroot
1–2 fresh green chilies, seeded and chopped
1 tbsp paprika
2 tsp ground coriander
1 tbsp mild or medium curry powder
2 cups vegetable stock
14 oz/400 g canned chopped tomatoes
1 green bell pepper, seeded and sliced
1 tbsp cornstarch
⅔ cup coconut milk
2–3 tbsp ground almonds
salt
fresh cilantro sprigs, to garnish
freshly cooked rice, to serve

Cut the eggplant, turnips, and potatoes into ½-inch/1-cm cubes. Break the cauliflower into small florets. Leave the mushrooms whole if small or slice them thickly, if preferred. Slice the onion and carrots.

Heat the ghee in a large pan over low heat. Add the onion, turnips, potatoes, and cauliflower and cook, stirring frequently, for 3 minutes.

Add the garlic, ginger, chili, paprika, ground coriander, and curry powder and cook, stirring constantly, for 1 minute.

Add the stock, tomatoes, eggplant, and mushrooms and season to taste with salt. Cover and simmer, stirring occasionally, for 30 minutes, or until tender. Add the green bell pepper and carrots, cover and cook for another 5 minutes.

Put the cornstarch and coconut milk in a bowl, mix into a smooth paste, and stir into the vegetable mixture. Add the ground almonds and let simmer, stirring constantly, for 2 minutes. Taste and adjust the seasoning, if necessary. Transfer to serving plates, garnish with cilantro sprigs, and serve immediately with freshly cooked rice.

serves 4 | prep 20 mins | cook 40 mins

vegetable korma

INGREDIENTS
4 tbsp ghee or vegetable oil
2 onions, chopped
2 garlic cloves, chopped
1 fresh red chili, chopped
1 tbsp grated fresh gingerroot
2 tomatoes, peeled and chopped
1 orange bell pepper, seeded and cut into
** small pieces**
1 large potato, cut into chunks
7 oz/200 g cauliflower florets
½ tsp salt
1 tsp turmeric
1 tsp ground cumin
1 tsp ground coriander
1 tsp garam masala
scant 1 cup vegetable stock or water
⅔ cup plain yogurt
⅔ cup light cream
1 oz/25 g fresh cilantro, chopped
freshly cooked rice, to serve

Heat the ghee in a large pan over medium heat, add the onions and garlic, and cook, stirring frequently, for 3 minutes. Add the chili and ginger and cook for an additional 4 minutes. Add the tomatoes, orange bell pepper, potato, cauliflower, salt, and spices and cook, stirring constantly, for another 3 minutes. Stir in the stock and bring to a boil. Reduce the heat and simmer for 25 minutes.

Stir in the yogurt and cream and cook, stirring frequently, for an additional 5 minutes without boiling. Add the fresh cilantro and heat through.

Serve with freshly cooked rice.

serves 4 | prep 15 mins, plus 1 hr chilling | cook 12–15 mins

spinach & ricotta dumplings

INGREDIENTS
**2 lb 4 oz/1 kg fresh spinach leaves, tough stalks
removed**
1½ cups ricotta cheese
1 cup freshly grated Parmesan cheese
3 eggs, lightly beaten
pinch of freshly grated nutmeg
**¾–1¼ cups all-purpose flour, plus extra
for dusting**
salt and pepper

HERB BUTTER
½ cup unsalted butter
2 tbsp chopped fresh oregano
2 tbsp chopped fresh sage

Wash the spinach, then put in a pan with just the water clinging to its leaves. Cover and cook over low heat for 6–8 minutes until just wilted. Drain well and let cool.

Squeeze or press out as much liquid as possible from the spinach, then finely chop or process in a food processor. Put the spinach in a bowl and add the ricotta, half the Parmesan cheese, the eggs, nutmeg, and salt and pepper to taste. Beat until thoroughly combined. Sift in ¾ cup of the flour and lightly work it into the mixture, adding more, if necessary, to make a workable mixture. Cover with plastic wrap and let chill in the refrigerator for 1 hour.

With floured hands, break off small pieces of the mixture and roll into walnut-size balls.

Handle them as little as possible, as they are quite delicate. Lightly dust the dumplings with flour.

Bring a large pan of lightly salted water to a boil. Add the dumplings and cook for 2–3 minutes until they rise to the surface. Remove with a slotted spoon, drain well, and set aside.

Meanwhile, make the herb butter. Melt the butter in a large, heavy-bottom skillet over low heat. Add the oregano and sage and cook, stirring frequently, for 1 minute. Add the dumplings and toss gently for 1 minute to coat. Transfer to a warmed serving dish, sprinkle with the remaining Parmesan cheese, and serve immediately.

serves 4 | prep 20 mins, plus 10 mins' cooling | cook 1¼ hrs

vegetable & hazelnut loaf

INGREDIENTS

2 tbsp sunflower-seed oil, plus extra for oiling
1 onion, chopped
1 garlic clove, finely chopped
2 celery stalks, chopped
1 tbsp all-purpose flour
scant 1 cup strained canned tomatoes
2 cups fresh whole wheat bread crumbs
2 carrots, grated
¾ cup toasted hazelnuts, ground
1 tbsp dark soy sauce
2 tbsp chopped fresh cilantro
1 egg, lightly beaten
salt and pepper

Put the bread crumbs, carrots, ground hazelnuts, soy sauce, and cilantro in a bowl. Add the tomato mixture and stir well. Let cool slightly, then beat in the egg and season to taste with salt and pepper.

Spoon the mixture into the prepared pan and smooth the surface. Cover with foil and bake in the preheated oven for 1 hour. If serving hot, turn the loaf out onto a warmed serving dish and serve immediately. Alternatively, let cool in the pan before turning out.

Preheat the oven to 350°F/180°C. Oil and line a 1-lb/450-g loaf pan. Heat the oil in a heavy-bottom skillet over medium heat. Add the onion and cook, stirring frequently, for 5 minutes, or until softened. Add the garlic and celery and cook, stirring frequently, for 5 minutes. Add the flour and cook, stirring constantly, for 1 minute. Gradually stir in the strained canned tomatoes and cook, stirring constantly, until thickened. Remove the skillet from the heat.

VARIATION

For a different presentation, you can cook the loaf in a round cake pan and serve in wedges.

serves 4 | prep 10 mins | cook 45 mins

cauliflower bake

INGREDIENTS
1 lb 2 oz/500 g cauliflower, broken into florets
1 lb 5 oz/600 g potatoes, cut into cubes
3½ oz/100 g cherry tomatoes

SAUCE
2 tbsp butter or margarine
1 leek, sliced
1 garlic clove, crushed
3 tbsp all-purpose flour
1¼ cups milk
3 oz/85 g mixed cheese, such as Cheddar,
  Parmesan, and Gruyère, grated
½ tsp paprika
2 tbsp chopped fresh flat-leaf parsley,
  plus extra to garnish
salt and pepper

Preheat the oven to 350°F/180°C. Bring a large pan of salted water to a boil, add the cauliflower, and cook for 10 minutes. Meanwhile, bring a separate large pan of salted water to a boil, add the potatoes, and cook for 10 minutes. Drain both vegetables and set aside.

To make the sauce, melt the butter in a large pan, add the leek and garlic, and cook over low heat for 1 minute. Stir in the flour and cook, stirring constantly, for 1 minute. Remove from the heat, then gradually stir in the milk, ½ cup of the cheese, the paprika, and parsley. Return to the heat and bring to a boil, stirring constantly. Season to taste with salt and pepper.

Transfer the cauliflower to a deep, ovenproof dish with the tomatoes, and top with the potatoes. Pour the sauce over the potatoes and sprinkle over the remaining cheese.

Cook in the preheated oven for 20 minutes, or until the vegetables are cooked through and the cheese is golden brown and bubbling. Garnish with chopped parsley and serve immediately.

VARIATION
You can use broccoli instead of cauliflower for this dish, if you prefer. Alternatively, use a mixture of broccoli and cauliflower for a combination of colors.

serves 4–6 | prep 10 mins | cook 1 hr 5 mins

tomato & onion bake with eggs

INGREDIENTS
4 tbsp butter, plus extra for greasing
2 large onions, thinly sliced
1 lb 2 oz/500 g tomatoes, peeled and sliced
2 cups fresh white bread crumbs
4 eggs
salt and pepper

Preheat the oven to 350°F/180°C. Grease an ovenproof dish.

Melt 3 tablespoons of the butter in a heavy-bottom skillet over low heat. Add the onions and cook, stirring frequently, for 5 minutes, or until softened.

Layer the onions, tomatoes, and bread crumbs in the prepared dish, seasoning each layer with salt and pepper to taste. Dot the remaining butter on top. Bake in the preheated oven for 40 minutes.

Remove the bake from the oven and make 4 hollows in the mixture with the back of a spoon. Crack 1 egg into each hollow. Return the dish to the oven for an additional 15 minutes, or until the eggs are just set. Serve immediately.

VARIATION
For added spice, seed and slice
2 red bell peppers and add
once the onions have softened.
Cook for 10 minutes, then stir
in a pinch of cayenne pepper.

serves 4 | prep 15 mins | cook 40 mins

vegetable crumble

INGREDIENTS

1 cauliflower, cut into florets
2 tbsp sunflower-seed oil
scant ¼ cup all-purpose flour
1½ cups milk
11½ oz/325 g canned corn kernels, drained
2 tbsp chopped fresh parsley
1 tsp chopped fresh thyme
5 oz/140 g Cheddar cheese, grated
salt and pepper

TOPPING

scant ½ cup whole wheat flour
2 tbsp butter
⅓ cup rolled oats
scant ¼ cup blanched almonds, chopped

Preheat the oven to 375°F/190°C. Bring a large pan of lightly salted water to a boil, add the cauliflower, and cook for 5 minutes. Drain well, reserving the cooking liquid. Heat the oil in a pan over medium heat and stir in the flour. Cook, stirring constantly, for 1 minute. Remove from the heat and gradually stir in the milk and ⅔ cup of the reserved cooking liquid. Return to the heat and bring to a boil, stirring constantly. Cook,

stirring, for 3 minutes, or until thickened. Remove from the heat.

Stir the corn, parsley, thyme, and half the cheese into the sauce and season to taste with salt and pepper. Fold in the cauliflower, then spoon the mixture into an ovenproof dish.

To make the crumble topping, put the flour in a bowl, add the butter, and rub into the flour with your fingertips until the mixture resembles bread crumbs. Stir in the oats and almonds, add the remaining cheese, then sprinkle the mixture evenly over the vegetables. Bake in the preheated oven for 30 minutes. Serve immediately.

VARIATION

For extra color, replace half the cauliflower with fresh green broccoli at the beginning of the recipe.

serves 4–6 | prep 20 mins, plus 10 mins' standing | cook 45 mins

mixed vegetable stew

INGREDIENTS

about ½ cup olive oil

2 large onions, thinly sliced

4 large garlic cloves, crushed

10½ oz/300 g eggplant, cut into
** ½-inch/1-cm cubes**

10½ oz/300 g yellow or green zucchini, cut into
** ½-inch/1-cm cubes**

1 large red bell pepper, seeded and chopped

1 large yellow bell pepper, seeded and chopped

1 large green bell pepper, seeded and chopped

2 fresh thyme sprigs

1 bay leaf

1 small, young fresh rosemary sprig

generous ⅓ cup vegetable stock

1 lb/450 g large, juicy tomatoes, peeled,
** seeded and chopped**

salt and pepper

fresh basil or oregano sprigs, to garnish

Heat about 2 tablespoons of the oil in a large, ovenproof casserole over medium heat. Add the onions and cook, stirring frequently, for 5 minutes, or until softened but not browned. Add the garlic and cook, stirring, for 1 minute. Reduce the heat to very low.

Meanwhile, heat a skillet over high heat until you can feel the heat rising. Add 1 tablespoon of the remaining oil and the eggplant cubes to make a single layer. Cook, stirring, until slightly brown on all sides. Transfer to the casserole with the onions.

Heat an additional tablespoon of the remaining oil in the skillet. Add the zucchini and cook, stirring, until lightly browned all over. Transfer to the casserole. Heat another tablespoon of the remaining oil in the pan, add the bell peppers, and cook, stirring, until soft. Transfer to the casserole.

Stir the thyme, bay leaf, rosemary, stock, and salt and pepper to taste into the casserole and bring to a boil. Reduce the heat to very low, cover, and simmer, stirring occasionally, for 20 minutes, or until the vegetables are tender and blended.

Remove from the heat and stir in the tomatoes. Cover and set aside for 10 minutes for the tomatoes to soften. Serve, or let cool completely and then serve chilled the next day, garnished with basil or oregano sprigs.

serves 4 | prep 15 mins | cook 2¼–2½ hrs

provençal bean stew

INGREDIENTS

2 cups dried pinto beans,
  soaked overnight in water to cover

2 tbsp olive oil

2 onions, sliced

2 garlic cloves, finely chopped

1 red bell pepper, seeded and sliced

1 yellow bell pepper, seeded and sliced

14 oz/400 g canned chopped tomatoes

2 tbsp tomato paste

1 tbsp torn fresh basil leaves

2 tsp chopped fresh thyme

2 tsp chopped fresh rosemary

1 bay leaf

⅓ cup black olives, pitted and halved

salt and pepper

2 tbsp chopped fresh parsley, to garnish

Drain the beans. Place in a large pan, add enough cold water to cover, and bring to a boil. Reduce the heat, then cover and let simmer for 1¼–1½ hours until almost tender. Drain, reserving 1¼ cups of the cooking liquid.

Heat the oil in a heavy-bottom pan over medium heat. Add the onions and cook, stirring frequently, for 5 minutes, or until softened. Add the garlic and bell peppers and cook, stirring occasionally, for 10 minutes.

Add the tomatoes and their can juices, the reserved cooking liquid, tomato paste, basil, thyme, rosemary, bay leaf, and beans. Season to taste with salt and pepper. Cover and simmer for 40 minutes. Add the olives and simmer for 5 minutes. Transfer to a warmed serving dish, sprinkle with the parsley, and serve immediately.

COOK'S TIP

When using beans, always follow the package instructions for soaking and cooking. If you use cranberry or red kidney beans, boil them vigorously for 15 minutes before simmering.

serves 4 | prep 20 mins | cook 1¼ hrs

vegetable chili

INGREDIENTS

1 eggplant, cut into 1-inch/2.5-cm slices

1 tbsp olive oil, plus extra for brushing

1 large red or yellow onion, finely chopped

2 red or yellow bell peppers, seeded
  and finely chopped

3–4 garlic cloves, finely chopped or crushed

1 lb 12 oz/800 g canned chopped tomatoes

1 tbsp mild chili powder

½ tsp ground cumin

½ tsp dried oregano

2 small zucchini, quartered lengthwise
  and sliced

14 oz/400 g canned kidney beans, drained
  and rinsed

2 cups water

1 tbsp tomato paste

6 scallions, finely chopped

4 oz/115 g Cheddar cheese, grated

salt and pepper

Brush the eggplant slices on one side with oil. Heat half the oil in a large, heavy-bottom skillet over medium heat. Add the eggplant slices, oiled-side up, and cook for 5–6 minutes, or until browned on one side. Turn the slices over and cook on the other side until browned, then transfer to a plate. Cut into bite-size pieces.

Heat the remaining oil in a large pan over medium heat. Add the onion and bell peppers and cook, stirring frequently, for 3–4 minutes until the onion is just softened. Add the garlic and cook, stirring frequently, for an additional 2–3 minutes until the onion is beginning to color.

Add the tomatoes, chili powder, cumin, and oregano and season to taste with salt and pepper. Bring just to a boil, then reduce the heat, cover, and let simmer gently for 15 minutes.

Add the zucchini, eggplant pieces, beans, water, and tomato paste to the pan and return to a boil. Reduce the heat, cover, and let simmer for an additional 45 minutes, or until the vegetables are tender. Taste and adjust the seasoning, if necessary.

Ladle into warmed bowls and top with the scallions and cheese.

COOK'S TIP

If you would prefer to leave the purple eggplant skin out of this chili, you can peel the eggplant before cutting it into slices.

serves 6 | prep 20 mins | cook 1 hr 40 mins–2 hrs

mexican three-bean chili hotchpotch

INGREDIENTS

generous ¾ cup each dried black beans,
  cannellini beans and pinto beans, soaked
  overnight in separate bowls in water to cover
2 tbsp olive oil
1 large onion, finely chopped
2 red bell peppers, seeded and diced
2 garlic cloves, very finely chopped
½ tsp cumin seeds, crushed
1 tsp coriander seeds, crushed
1 tsp dried oregano
½–2 tsp chili powder
3 tbsp tomato paste
1 lb 12 oz/800 g canned chopped tomatoes
1 tsp sugar
1 tsp salt
2½ cups vegetable stock
3 tbsp chopped fresh cilantro

Drain the beans, put in separate pans, and cover with cold water. Bring to a boil and boil vigorously for 10–15 minutes, then reduce the heat and let simmer for 35–45 minutes until just tender. Drain and set aside.

Heat the oil in a large, heavy-bottom pan over medium heat. Add the onion and bell peppers and cook, stirring frequently, for 5 minutes, or until softened.

Add the garlic, cumin, and coriander seeds and oregano and cook, stirring, for 30 seconds until the garlic is beginning to color. Add the chili powder and tomato paste and cook, stirring, for 1 minute. Add the tomatoes, sugar, salt, beans, and stock.

Bring to a boil, then reduce the heat, cover, and let simmer, stirring occasionally, for 45 minutes.

Stir in the fresh cilantro. Ladle into individual warmed bowls and serve immediately.

serves 4 | prep 20 mins | cook 50 mins–1 hr

vegetable moussaka

INGREDIENTS
about ½ cup olive oil
1 onion, chopped
4 celery stalks, chopped
1 garlic clove, finely chopped
14 oz/400 g canned chopped tomatoes
10½ oz/300 g canned green lentils
2 tbsp chopped fresh parsley
1 large eggplant, sliced
salt and pepper

SAUCE
2 tbsp butter
scant ¼ cup all-purpose flour
1¼ cups milk
pinch of freshly grated nutmeg
1 egg
½ cup freshly grated Parmesan cheese

Preheat the oven to 350°F/180°C. Heat
1 tablespoon of the oil in a skillet over medium
heat. Add the onion and cook, stirring frequently,
for 5 minutes, or until softened. Add the celery,
garlic, tomatoes, lentils and their can juices, and
parsley. Season to taste with salt and pepper.
Reduce the heat, cover, and let simmer gently,
stirring occasionally, for 15 minutes, or until the
mixture has thickened.

Meanwhile, heat a little of the remaining oil in a
large, heavy-bottom skillet. Add the eggplant
slices, in batches if necessary, and cook until
golden on both sides, adding more oil as
necessary. Remove with a slotted spoon and drain
on paper towels. Layer an ovenproof dish with the

lentil and tomato mixture and the eggplant slices,
ending with a layer of eggplant.

To make the sauce, put the butter, flour, and milk
in a pan over medium–low heat and bring to a boil,
whisking constantly. Season to taste with salt and
pepper and nutmeg. Remove from the heat, let
cool slightly, then beat in the egg. Pour the sauce
over the eggplant, sprinkle with the Parmesan
cheese, and bake in the preheated oven for
30–40 minutes until golden on top. Serve
immediately.

VARIATION
*For the traditional meat-
eaters' version of this dish,
substitute 1¹/₂ cups fresh
ground lamb for the lentils.
Brown with the onions for
10 minutes.*

serves 4 | prep 10 mins, plus 30 mins' soaking | cook 40 mins

vegetable lasagna

INGREDIENTS
⅜ **cup dried porcini mushrooms**
2 tbsp olive oil
1 onion, finely chopped
14 oz/400 g canned chopped tomatoes
4 tbsp butter, plus extra for greasing
1 lb/450 g white mushrooms, thinly sliced
1 garlic clove, finely chopped
1 tbsp lemon juice
½ tsp Dijon mustard
¾ quantity cheese sauce
6 sheets no-precook lasagna
½ cup freshly grated Parmesan cheese
salt and pepper

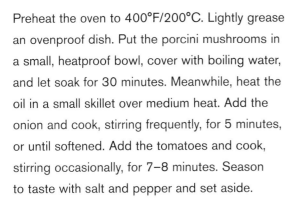

Preheat the oven to 400°F/200°C. Lightly grease an ovenproof dish. Put the porcini mushrooms in a small, heatproof bowl, cover with boiling water, and let soak for 30 minutes. Meanwhile, heat the oil in a small skillet over medium heat. Add the onion and cook, stirring frequently, for 5 minutes, or until softened. Add the tomatoes and cook, stirring occasionally, for 7–8 minutes. Season to taste with salt and pepper and set aside.

Drain and slice the porcini mushrooms. Melt half the butter in a large, heavy-bottom skillet over medium heat. Add the porcini and white mushrooms and cook, stirring, until they begin to release their juices. Reduce the heat to low, add the garlic and lemon juice, and season to taste with salt and pepper. Cook, stirring occasionally, until almost all the liquid has evaporated.

Stir the mustard into the cheese sauce, then spread a layer over the base of the dish. Arrange a layer of lasagna sheets on top, cover with the mushrooms, another layer of sauce, another layer of lasagna, the tomato mixture and, finally, another layer of sauce. Sprinkle with the Parmesan cheese and dot with the remaining butter.

Bake in the preheated oven for 20 minutes. Let stand for 5 minutes before serving.

COOK'S TIP
Instead of grating the Parmesan cheese, you can shave off very thin strips using a vegetable peeler, to give a different consistency to the topping.

5

Salads are not just for summery days—with the wide variety of different-flavored and textured leaves freely available, you can enjoy them all year round. Salad greens are particularly good with cheese, and here we have peppery arugula paired with smoked mozzarella slices and crisp romaine with coarsely grated Parmesan.

SALADS

But traditional salad ingredients are only part of the picture. A range of vegetables and nuts are also imaginatively combined—zucchini with pine nuts, beet with pecans, as well as green beans with walnuts. And fruit, too, makes an exciting culinary contribution in the vibrant Orange & Fennel Salad and the refreshing Pineapple & Cucumber Salad.

serves 4 | prep 15 mins | no cooking required

greek salad

INGREDIENTS
4 tomatoes, cut into wedges
1 onion, sliced
½ cucumber, sliced
1½ cups kalamata olives, stoned
8 oz/225 g feta cheese, cubed
2 tbsp fresh cilantro leaves
fresh flat-leaf parsley sprigs, to garnish
pita bread, to serve

DRESSING
5 tbsp extra virgin olive oil
2 tbsp white wine vinegar
1 tbsp lemon juice
½ tsp sugar
1 tbsp chopped fresh cilantro
salt and pepper

To make the dressing, put all the ingredients for the dressing into a large bowl and mix well together.

Add the tomatoes, onion, cucumber, olives, cheese, and cilantro. Toss all the ingredients together, then divide between individual serving bowls. Garnish with parsley sprigs and serve with pita bread.

serves 4–6 | prep 10 mins, plus 3½ hrs' chilling | cook 10 mins

moorish zucchini salad

INGREDIENTS
about 4 tbsp olive oil
1 large garlic clove, halved
1 lb 2 oz/500 g small zucchini, thinly sliced
⅜ cup pine nuts
⅓ cup raisins
3 tbsp finely chopped fresh mint leaves
  (not spearmint or peppermint)
about 2 tbsp lemon juice, or to taste
salt and pepper

Heat the oil in a large skillet over medium heat. Add the garlic and cook for 5 minutes, or until golden, to flavor the oil. Remove with a slotted spoon and discard. Add the zucchini and cook, stirring frequently, for 5 minutes, or until just tender. Immediately remove with a slotted spoon and transfer to a large serving bowl.

Add the pine nuts, raisins, mint, lemon juice, and salt and pepper to taste to the zucchini and carefully stir to mix. Taste and add more oil, lemon juice and seasoning, if necessary.

Let cool completely, then cover with plastic wrap and chill in the refrigerator for at least 3¹/₂ hours. Remove the salad from the refrigerator 10 minutes before serving.

COOK'S TIP
This salad is best made with young, tender zucchini no more than 1 inch/2.5 cm thick. If using older, larger zucchini, cut them in half or quarters lengthwise first, then slice thinly.

serves 4 | prep 5 mins | cook 15 mins

warm potatoes with pesto

INGREDIENTS
1 lb/450 g small new potatoes
3 tsp pesto sauce
¼ cup fresh grated Parmesan cheese
salt and pepper

Bring a large pan of salted water to a boil. Add the potatoes and cook for 15 minutes, or until tender. Drain, transfer to a salad bowl, and let cool slightly.

Add the pesto sauce and salt and pepper to taste to the potatoes and toss together. Sprinkle with the Parmesan cheese and serve warm.

serves 4 | prep 15 mins | no cooking required

mozzarella salad with sun-dried tomatoes

INGREDIENTS

⅝ **cup sun-dried tomatoes in olive oil**
  (drained weight), oil from the jar reserved
½ **oz/15 g fresh basil, coarsely shredded**
½ **oz/15 g fresh flat-leaf parsley, coarsely chopped**
1 **tbsp capers, rinsed**
1 **tbsp balsamic vinegar**
1 **garlic clove, coarsely chopped**
extra olive oil, if necessary
3½ **oz/100 g mixed salad greens, such as oak leaf**
  lettuce, baby spinach, and arugula
1 **lb 2 oz/500 g smoked mozzarella, sliced**
pepper

Put the sun-dried tomatoes, basil, parsley, capers, vinegar, and garlic in a food processor. Measure the oil from the sun-dried tomatoes jar and make it up to ⅔ cup with more olive oil, if necessary. Add it to the food processor and process until smooth. Season to taste with pepper.

Divide the salad greens between 4 individual serving plates. Top with the slices of mozzarella and spoon over the dressing. Serve immediately.

VARIATION

Substitute Taleggio or a soft goat milk cheese for the mozzarella.

serves 4 | prep 15 mins | cook 10–15 mins

italian salad

INGREDIENTS
8 oz/225 g dried conchiglie
⅓ cup pine nuts
12 oz/350 g cherry tomatoes, halved
1 red bell pepper, seeded and cut into
  bite-size chunks
1 red onion, chopped
7 oz/200 g mozzarella di bufala, cut into
  small pieces
12 black olives, pitted
1 oz/25 g fresh basil leaves
fresh Parmesan cheese shavings, to garnish

DRESSING
5 tbsp extra virgin olive oil
2 tbsp balsamic vinegar
1 tbsp chopped fresh basil
salt and pepper

Bring a large pan of lightly salted water to a boil. Add the pasta, return to a boil, and cook for 8–10 minutes until tender but still firm to the bite. Drain, refresh under cold running water, and drain again. Let cool.

Meanwhile, heat a dry skillet over low heat, add the pine nuts, and cook, shaking the skillet frequently, for 1–2 minutes until lightly toasted. Remove from the heat, transfer to a dish, and let cool.

To make the dressing, put all the ingredients for the dressing in a small bowl and mix well together. Cover with plastic wrap, and set aside.

To assemble the salad, divide the pasta between 4 serving bowls. Add the pine nuts, tomatoes, bell pepper, onion, cheese, and olives. Sprinkle over the basil, then drizzle over the dressing. Garnish with Parmesan cheese shavings and serve.

serves 4 | prep 10 mins | cook 15 mins

pasta salad with charbroiled bell peppers

INGREDIENTS

1 red bell pepper
1 orange bell pepper
10 oz/280 g dried conchiglie
5 tbsp extra virgin olive oil
2 tbsp lemon juice
2 tbsp pesto sauce
1 garlic clove
3 tbsp shredded fresh basil leaves
salt and pepper

Preheat the broiler to medium–high. Arrange the bell peppers on a baking sheet and broil, turning frequently, for 15 minutes, or until charred all over. Remove with tongs and transfer to a bowl. Cover with crumpled paper towels and set aside.

Meanwhile, bring a large pan of lightly salted water to a boil. Add the pasta, return to a boil, and cook for 8–10 minutes until tender but still firm to the bite.

Combine the oil, lemon juice, pesto sauce, and garlic in a large bowl, whisking well to mix. Drain the pasta, add it to the pesto mixture while still hot, and toss well. Set aside.

When the bell peppers are cool enough to handle, peel off the skins. Halve, then remove and discard the seeds. Coarsely chop the flesh and add to the pasta with the basil. Season to taste with salt and pepper and toss well. Serve at room temperature.

VARIATION

A more traditional salad, without the pasta, can be made in the same way. When the bell peppers have been under the broiler for 10 minutes, add 4 tomatoes and broil for an additional 5 minutes. Cover the bell peppers with paper towels, then peel and chop. Peel and coarsely chop the tomatoes. Combine them with the dressing and garnish with black olives.

serves 4 | prep 5 mins | cook 5 mins

hot-&-sour noodle salad

INGREDIENTS
12 oz/350 g dried rice vermicelli noodles
4 tbsp sesame oil
3 tbsp soy sauce
juice of 2 limes
1 tsp sugar
4 scallions, finely sliced
1–2 tsp hot chili sauce
2 tbsp chopped fresh cilantro

Prepare the noodles according to the package instructions. Drain, put in a bowl and toss with half the oil.

Mix the remaining oil, soy sauce, lime juice, sugar, scallions, and chili sauce together in a bowl. Stir into the noodles.

Stir in the cilantro and serve.

serves 4 | prep 15 mins, plus 1 hr chilling | cook 5 mins

cauliflower & olive salad

INGREDIENTS

1 large cauliflower
1⅓ cups pitted black olives, chopped
2 pimientos, chopped
2 tomatoes (optional)

DRESSING
¾ cup vegetable oil
3 tbsp white wine vinegar
1 garlic clove, crushed
salt and pepper

Break the cauliflower into florets. Bring a large pan of salted water to a boil. Add the cauliflower and cook for 5 minutes, or until just tender. Drain well.

Combine the cauliflower, olives, and pimientos in a large bowl. If using tomatoes, quarter, seed, and chop the flesh. Add to the bowl with the other ingredients.

Put all the dressing ingredients in a screw-top jar and shake well. Pour the dressing over the salad and toss gently to coat. Cover with plastic wrap and let chill in the refrigerator for at least 1 hour.

Remove from the refrigerator 10 minutes before serving. Stir once more, then transfer to a dish and serve.

serves 4 | prep 15 mins, plus 20 mins' cooling | cook 20 mins

caesar salad

INGREDIENTS

1 garlic clove, halved

1 romaine lettuce, separated into leaves

½ cup coarsely grated Parmesan cheese

2 eggs (optional)

GARLIC CROUTONS

3 tbsp olive oil

1 large garlic clove, halved

4 slices whole wheat bread, crusts removed,
 cut into cubes

DRESSING

1 egg (or 1 tbsp sour cream)

1 tsp vegetarian Worcestershire sauce

2 tbsp lemon juice

2 tsp Dijon mustard

2 tbsp olive oil

salt and pepper

Preheat the oven to 375°F/190°C. To make the croutons, heat the oil with the garlic in a small pan over low heat for 5 minutes. Remove and discard the garlic. Put the bread cubes in a bowl, pour in the oil, and toss to coat. Spread the cubes out on a baking sheet. Bake in the preheated oven for 10 minutes, or until crisp. Remove from the oven and let cool.

To make the dressing, put the egg in a pan of water, bring to a boil, and boil for 1 minute. Remove with a slotted spoon. Crack the egg into a bowl, scooping out any remaining egg white from the shell. Whisk in the Worcestershire sauce, lemon juice, mustard, and oil and season to taste with salt and pepper.

Rub the inside of a salad bowl with the garlic halves, then discard. Arrange the lettuce leaves in the salad bowl and sprinkle with the Parmesan cheese. Add hard-cooked eggs, if desired. Drizzle the dressing over the salad and sprinkle the garlic croutons on top. Toss the salad at the table and serve.

VARIATION

Add a pinch of cayenne pepper and 1 teaspoon of paprika to the oil before you bake the croutons.

COOK'S TIP

For children, invalids, and pregnant women, substitute sour cream for the lightly cooked egg in the dressing and add quartered hard-cooked eggs to the salad.

serves 4 | prep 15 mins, plus 4 hrs' chilling | no cooking required

nutty beet salad

INGREDIENTS

3 cooked beet, grated

3 tbsp red wine vinegar or fruit vinegar

2 tart apples, such as Granny Smith

2 tbsp lemon juice

DRESSING

4 tbsp plain yogurt

4 tbsp mayonnaise

1 garlic clove, chopped

1 tbsp chopped fresh dill

salt and pepper

TO SERVE

4 large handfuls of mixed salad greens

4 tbsp pecan halves

Put the beet in a nonmetallic dish and sprinkle with the vinegar. Cover with plastic wrap and let chill in the refrigerator for at least 4 hours.

Core and slice the apples. Put in a dish. Sprinkle with the lemon juice to prevent discoloration.

To make the dressing, combine all the dressing ingredients in a small bowl. Remove the beet from the refrigerator and drizzle over the dressing. Add the apples to the beet and mix gently to coat with the dressing.

To serve, arrange a handful of salad greens on each plate and top with a large spoonful of the apple and beet mixture.

Heat a dry skillet over medium heat, add the pecans, and cook, shaking the skillet frequently, for 2 minutes, or until they begin to brown. Sprinkle the toasted nuts over the salad and serve immediately.

serves 4 | prep 15 mins | no cooking required

good coleslaw

INGREDIENTS
½ hard white cabbage
2 carrots
2 eating apples
2 celery stalks
3 scallions
⅔ cup mayonnaise
⅔ cup plain yogurt
1 tsp French mustard
2 tbsp lemon juice
generous ¼ cup raisins (optional)
⅜ cup walnuts (optional)

Finely shred the cabbage. Grate the carrots and core and slice the apples. Finely chop the celery and scallions. Put in a large bowl.

Mix the mayonnaise and yogurt together in a small bowl. Whisk in the mustard and lemon juice and season well with salt and pepper.

Add the raisins and walnuts to the salad vegetables, if using. Pour over the dressing and mix well. Serve immediately.

serves 2 as an appetizer or 4 as a side dish | prep 10 mins, plus 30 mins' chilling | cook 5 mins

green bean & walnut salad

INGREDIENTS

1 lb/450 g green beans
1 small onion, finely chopped
1 garlic clove, chopped
4 tbsp freshly grated Parmesan cheese,
  plus extra to garnish
2 tbsp chopped walnuts or almonds, to garnish

DRESSING
6 tbsp olive oil
2 tbsp white wine vinegar
2 tsp chopped fresh tarragon
salt and pepper

Trim the beans, but leave them whole. Bring a pan of salted water to a boil. Add the beans and cook for 3–4 minutes. Drain well, refresh under cold running water, and drain again. Put in a large bowl and add the onion, garlic, and cheese.

Put all the dressing ingredients in a screw-top jar and shake well. Pour the dressing over the salad and toss gently to coat. Cover with plastic wrap and chill in the refrigerator for at least 30 minutes.

Remove from the refrigerator 10 minutes before serving. Give the beans a brief stir and transfer to a shallow serving dish.

Heat a dry skillet over medium heat, add the nuts, and cook, shaking the skillet frequently, for 2 minutes, or until they begin to brown. Sprinkle the toasted nuts and Parmesan cheese over the beans to garnish and serve immediately.

serves 6 | prep 15 mins | no cooking required

arugula & avocado salad

INGREDIENTS

1 red or green escarole lettuce, torn
½ frisée lettuce, torn
1 small bunch of watercress or mizuna
1 bunch of arugula, torn
1 red onion, thinly sliced into rings
2 oranges
1 avocado
½ cup walnuts, coarsely chopped

DRESSING

6 tbsp olive oil
1 tbsp walnut oil
3 tbsp fresh lemon juice
2 tbsp fresh orange juice
1 tsp finely grated orange rind
1 tsp Dijon mustard
pinch of sugar
salt and pepper

COOK'S TIP

Always make sure that salad greens are well dried after washing. Use a salad spinner, except for delicate leaves, or gently pat dry with paper towels or a dish towel.

To make the dressing, put all the ingredients for the dressing in a small bowl and whisk to mix.

Put the lettuces, watercress, and arugula in a salad bowl. Separate the onion rings and add to the bowl. Working over the bowl to catch the juice, peel the oranges with a sharp knife, and cut between the membranes to release the segments into the bowl.

Peel, pit, and dice the avocado. Add to the salad. Pour over the dressing and toss well to coat. Sprinkle the walnuts over the top and serve immediately.

VARIATION

For a milder nutty flavor, use ³/₈ cup toasted pine nuts in place of the chopped walnuts.

serves 4 | prep 15 mins | no cooking required

avocado salad with lime dressing

INGREDIENTS

2¼ oz/60 g mixed red and green lettuce leaves

2¼ oz/60 g wild arugula

4 scallions, finely diced

5 tomatoes, sliced

¼ cup walnuts, toasted and chopped

2 avocados

1 tbsp lemon juice

LIME DRESSING

1 tbsp lime juice

1 tsp French mustard

1 tbsp sour cream

1 tbsp chopped fresh parsley or cilantro

3 tbsp extra virgin olive oil

pinch of sugar

salt and pepper

Wash and drain the lettuce and arugula, if necessary. Shred all the leaves and arrange in the bottom of a large salad bowl. Add the scallions, tomatoes, and walnuts.

Peel, pit, and thinly slice or dice the avocados. Brush with the lemon juice to prevent discoloration, then transfer to the salad bowl. Gently mix together.

To make the dressing, put all the dressing ingredients in a screw-top jar and shake well. Drizzle over the salad and serve immediately.

serves 4 | prep 15 mins | no cooking required

orange & fennel salad

INGREDIENTS

4 large, juicy oranges
1 large fennel bulb, very thinly sliced
1 mild white onion, finely sliced
2 tbsp extra virgin olive oil
12 plump black olives, pitted and thinly sliced
1 fresh red chili, seeded and very
  thinly sliced (optional)
finely chopped fresh parsley
French bread, to serve

Finely grate the rind of the oranges into a bowl and set aside. Working over another bowl to catch the juice, use a small serrated knife to remove all the white pith from the oranges. Cut the oranges horizontally into thin slices.

Toss the orange slices with the fennel and onion slices in a large bowl. Whisk the oil into the reserved orange juice, then spoon over the oranges. Sprinkle the olive slices over the top, add the chili, if using, then sprinkle with the orange rind and parsley. Serve with French bread.

VARIATIONS

Garnet-red blood oranges look stunning.

Juicy dark grapes make an interesting alternative to the olives.

serves 4 | prep 20 mins | no cooking required

pineapple & cucumber salad

INGREDIENTS

1 cucumber

1 small fresh pineapple

1 red onion, thinly sliced

1 bunch of watercress

DRESSING

3 tbsp lemon juice

2 tbsp soy sauce

1 tsp sugar

1 tsp chili sauce

2 tbsp chopped fresh mint

Peel the cucumber and quarter lengthwise. Scoop out the seeds with a teaspoon and discard. Cut each quarter into ½-inch/1-cm pieces. Put in a large bowl.

Peel the pineapple and quarter lengthwise. Remove and discard the core. Cut each quarter in half lengthwise, then cut into ½-inch/1-cm pieces. Add to the cucumber. Add the onion and watercress and toss together.

To make the dressing, put all the dressing ingredients in a small bowl and whisk together.

Pour the dressing over the salad and toss together. Transfer to a large serving platter and serve immediately.

6

Nothing is more appealing to the taste buds than the contrast between a crumbly, buttery pie crust and a softly yielding vegetable filling, enriched with melting cheese or fluffy eggs, or both. Equally irresistible is a pizza fresh from the oven, with its crisp yet doughy base and piquant yet creamy topping.

TARTS, PIES & PIZZAS

Choose from a variety of pie crust experiences, from the traditional rich shortcrust and airy puff to the crunchy phyllo. Or try the unusual walnut- and Parmesan cheese-enhanced tart shells. For something truly out-of-the-ordinary, plump for the Mushroom Gougère, with its choux pastry shell. More familiar but no less delicious is the biscuit-style topping of Winter Vegetable Cobbler.

serves 4 | prep 30 mins, plus 45 mins' chilling and cooling | cook 1 hr

spring vegetable tart

INGREDIENTS

PIE DOUGH

1¾ cups all-purpose flour, plus extra for dusting

pinch of salt

9 tbsp cold butter, diced, plus extra
  for greasing

generous ⅓ cup grated Parmesan cheese

1 egg

ice-cold water

FILLING

10½ oz/300 g selection of baby spring vegetables,
  such as carrots, asparagus, peas, fava beans,
  salad onions, corn, and leeks

1¼ cups heavy cream

4½ oz/125 g sharp Cheddar cheese, grated

2 eggs plus 3 egg yolks

handful of tarragon and flat-leaf parsley, chopped

salt and pepper

Grease a 10-inch/25-cm loose-bottom tart pan. Sift the flour with the salt into a food processor, add the butter and process until the mixture resembles bread crumbs. Tip into a large bowl and add the Parmesan cheese. Mix the egg and water together in a small bowl. Add most of the egg mixture and combine with a round-bladed knife or your fingertips to form a soft dough, adding more if necessary. Turn out onto a lightly floured counter, roll out to 3¼ inches/8 cm larger than the pan and use to line the pan. Roll the rolling pin over the pan to neaten and trim the edge. Line the tart shell with parchment paper and fill with dried beans. Chill for 30 minutes. Meanwhile, preheat the oven to 400°F/200°C.

Bake the tart shell in the preheated oven for 15 minutes. Remove the paper and beans and bake for an additional 5 minutes. Remove from the oven and let cool. Reduce the oven temperature to 350°F/180°C.

Prepare the vegetables where necessary, then cut into bite-size pieces. Bring a large pan of lightly salted water to a boil. Add the vegetables and blanch for 2 minutes. Drain and let cool. Put the cream in a separate pan and bring to simmering point. Put the cheese, eggs, and egg yolks in a heatproof bowl and pour over the hot cream. Add the herbs and salt and pepper to taste and stir to combine. Arrange the vegetables in the tart shell, pour over the cheese custard, and bake for 30–40 minutes until just set. Let cool in the pan for 10 minutes before serving.

COOK'S TIP

Use only the most tender of young vegetables for this tart. If they are really small, you can leave them whole. A few slices of soft goat cheese can be added just before baking.

serves 4 | prep 40 mins, plus 1 hr chilling and cooling | cook 1¼ hrs

mushroom & onion quiche

INGREDIENTS
butter, for greasing
1 quantity rich shortcrust pie dough, chilled
all-purpose flour, for dusting

FILLING
4 tbsp unsalted butter
3 red onions, halved and sliced
12 oz/350 g mixed wild mushrooms, such as
  cèpes, chanterelles, and morels
2 tsp chopped fresh thyme
1 egg
2 egg yolks
generous ⅓ cup heavy cream
salt and pepper

Preheat the oven to 375°F/190°C. Lightly grease a 9-inch/23-cm loose-bottom quiche pan. Roll out the dough on a lightly floured counter and use to line the pan. Line the pastry shell with parchment paper and fill with dried beans. Chill in the refrigerator for 30 minutes. Bake in the preheated oven for 25 minutes. Remove the paper and beans and cool on a wire rack. Reduce the oven temperature to 350°F/180°C.

To make the filling, melt the butter in a large, heavy-bottom skillet over very low heat. Add the onions, cover, and cook, stirring occasionally, for 20 minutes. Add the mushrooms and thyme and cook, stirring occasionally, for an additional 10 minutes. Spoon into the pastry shell and put the pan on a baking sheet.

Lightly beat the egg, egg yolks, cream, and salt and pepper to taste in a bowl. Pour over the mushroom mixture. Bake in the oven for 20 minutes, or until the filling is set and golden. Serve hot or at room temperature.

COOK'S TIP
If you are in a hurry, you can use ready-prepared shortcrust pie dough, but if it is frozen, make sure that you thaw it thoroughly before use.

VARIATION
Try making this quiche with other mushrooms, such as shiitake, portobello, or oyster mushrooms.

serves 4 | prep 15 mins | cook 25 mins

potato, fontina & rosemary tart

INGREDIENTS
1 quantity puff pastry
all-purpose flour, for dusting

FILLING
3–4 waxy potatoes
10½ oz/300 g fontina cheese, cut into cubes
1 red onion, thinly sliced
3 large fresh rosemary sprigs
2 tbsp olive oil
1 egg yolk
salt and pepper

Preheat the oven to 375°F/190°C. Roll out the dough on a lightly floured counter into a circle about 10 inches/25 cm in diameter and put on a baking sheet.

Peel the potatoes and slice as thinly as possible so that they are almost transparent— use a mandolin if you have one. Arrange the potato slices in a spiral, overlapping the slices to cover the pastry, leaving a ¾-inch/2-cm margin around the edge.

Arrange the cheese and onion over the potatoes, sprinkle with the rosemary, and drizzle over the oil. Season to taste with salt and pepper and brush the edges with the egg yolk to glaze.

Bake in the preheated oven for 25 minutes, or until the potatoes are tender and the pastry is brown and crisp. Serve hot.

serves 4 | prep 30 mins | cook 1 hr

lattice tart

INGREDIENTS
butter, for greasing
2 quantities rich shortcrust pie dough,
 chilled
all-purpose flour, for dusting
lightly beaten egg, to glaze

FILLING
1 lb/450 g frozen spinach, thawed
2 tbsp olive oil
1 large onion, chopped
2 garlic cloves, finely chopped
2 eggs, lightly beaten
1 cup ricotta cheese
½ cup freshly grated Parmesan cheese
pinch of freshly grated nutmeg
salt and pepper

Preheat the oven to 400°F/200°C. To make the filling, drain the spinach and squeeze out as much moisture as possible. Heat the oil in a large, heavy-bottom skillet over medium heat. Add the onion and cook, stirring frequently, for 5 minutes, or until softened. Add the garlic and spinach and cook, stirring occasionally, for 10 minutes. Remove from the heat and let cool slightly, then beat in the eggs and the ricotta and Parmesan cheeses. Season to taste with salt and pepper and nutmeg.

Lightly grease a 9-inch/23-cm loose-bottom tart pan. Roll out two-thirds of the dough on a lightly floured counter and use to line the pan, leaving it overhanging the sides. Spoon in the spinach mixture, spreading it evenly over the base.

Roll out the remaining dough on a lightly floured counter and cut into ¼-inch/5-mm strips. Arrange the strips in a lattice pattern on top of the tart, pressing the ends securely to seal. Trim any excess dough. Brush with the egg to glaze and bake in the preheated oven for 45 minutes, or until golden brown. Transfer to a wire rack to cool slightly before removing from the pan.

COOK'S TIP
When preparing dough for a tart pan, roll out away from you lightly in one direction only. Rotate the dough in between strokes to ensure an even thickness.

makes 12 tartlets | prep 30 mins, plus 30 mins' chilling | cook 40 mins

stilton & walnut tartlets

INGREDIENTS

WALNUT PASTRY

1⅝ cups all-purpose flour, plus extra for dusting
pinch of celery salt
7 tbsp cold butter, diced, plus extra
    for greasing
¼ cup walnut halves, chopped
ice-cold water

FILLING

2 tbsp butter
2 celery stalks, finely chopped
1 small leek, finely chopped
scant 1 cup heavy cream plus 2 tbsp
7 oz/200 g Stilton cheese
3 egg yolks
salt and pepper
fresh parsley, to garnish

Lightly grease a 3-inch/7.5-cm, 12-hole muffin pan. Sift the flour with the celery salt into a food processor, add the butter, and process until the mixture resembles bread crumbs. Tip into a large bowl and add the walnuts and a little cold water, just enough to bring the dough together. Turn out onto a lightly floured counter and cut the dough in half. Roll out the first piece and cut out 6 x 3½-inch/9-cm circles. Roll out each circle to 4½ inches/12 cm in diameter and use to line the muffin holes. Repeat with the remaining dough. Line each hole with parchment paper and fill with dried beans. Chill in the refrigerator for 30 minutes. Meanwhile, preheat the oven to 400°F/200°C.

Bake the tartlet shells for 10 minutes. Remove from the oven, then remove the paper and beans.

To make the filling, melt the butter in a skillet over medium–low heat, add the celery and leek, and cook, stirring occasionally, for 15 minutes until very soft. Add the 2 tablespoons of cream, crumble in the cheese, and mix well. Season to taste with salt and pepper. Put the remaining cream in a pan and bring to simmering point. Pour onto the egg yolks in a heatproof bowl, stirring constantly. Mix in the cheese mixture and spoon into the tartlet shells. Bake for 10 minutes, then turn the pan around in the oven and bake for an additional 5 minutes. Let the tartlets cool in the pan for 5 minutes. Serve garnished with parsley.

serves 4–6 | prep 10 mins, plus 10 mins' resting | cook 45–50 mins

caramelized onion tart

INGREDIENTS
7 tbsp unsalted butter
1 lb 5 oz/600 g onions, thinly sliced
2 eggs
generous ⅓ cup heavy cream
⅞ cup grated Gruyère cheese
8-inch/20-cm ready-baked pastry shell
⅞ cup coarsely grated Parmesan cheese
salt and pepper

Melt the butter in a heavy-bottom skillet over medium heat. Add the onions and cook, stirring frequently to avoid burning, for 30 minutes, or until well-browned and caramelized. Remove the onions from the skillet and set aside.

Preheat the oven to 375°F/190°C. Beat the eggs in a large bowl, stir in the cream, and season to taste with salt and pepper. Add the Gruyère and mix well. Stir in the cooked onions.

Pour the egg and onion mixture into the baked pastry shell and sprinkle with the Parmesan cheese. Put on a baking sheet. Bake in the preheated oven for 15–20 minutes until the filling has set and begun to brown.

Remove from the oven and let rest for at least 10 minutes. The tart can be served hot or left to cool to room temperature.

serves 4 | prep 20 mins, plus 10 mins' cooling | cook 1 hr

mushroom gougère

INGREDIENTS

CHOUX PASTRY
½ **cup strong white bread flour**
pinch of salt
4 tbsp butter, plus extra for greasing
⅔ **cup water**
2 eggs
2 oz/55 g Emmental cheese, grated

FILLING
2 tbsp olive oil
1 onion, chopped
8 oz/225 g cremini mushrooms, sliced
2 garlic cloves, finely chopped
1 tbsp all-purpose flour
⅔ **cup vegetable stock**
¾ **cup walnuts, chopped**
2 tbsp chopped fresh parsley
salt and pepper

Preheat the oven to 400°F/200°C. To make the pastry, sift the flour with the salt onto a sheet of waxed paper. Melt the butter with the water in a pan over medium heat, but do not let the mixture boil. Add the flour all at once and beat vigorously with a wooden spoon until the mixture is smooth and comes away from the side of the pan. Remove from the heat, let cool for 10 minutes, then gradually beat in the eggs until smooth and glossy. Beat in the cheese. Grease a round ovenproof dish and spoon the pastry around the side.

To make the filling, heat the oil in a large, heavy-bottom skillet over medium heat. Add the onion and cook, stirring frequently, for 5 minutes, or until softened. Add the mushrooms and garlic and cook, stirring, for 2 minutes. Stir in the flour and cook, stirring constantly, for 1 minute. Gradually stir in the stock. Bring to a boil, stirring constantly, and cook for 3 minutes, or until thickened. Set aside 2 tablespoons of the walnuts. Stir the remainder into the mushroom mixture with the parsley. Season to taste with salt and pepper.

Spoon the filling into the center of the dish and sprinkle over the remaining walnuts. Bake in the preheated oven for 40 minutes, or until the pastry is risen and golden. Serve immediately.

serves 4 | prep 30 mins | cook 40 mins

winter vegetable cobbler

INGREDIENTS

1 tbsp olive oil
1 garlic clove, crushed
8 small onions, halved
2 celery stalks, sliced
8 oz/225 g rutabaga, chopped
2 carrots, sliced
½ small cauliflower, broken into florets
8 oz/225 g mushrooms, sliced
14 oz/400 g canned chopped tomatoes
¼ cup red split lentils, rinsed and drained
2 tbsp cornstarch
3–4 tbsp water
1¼ cups vegetable stock
2 tsp Tabasco sauce
2 tsp chopped fresh oregano, plus extra sprigs
  to garnish

TOPPING

1⅝ cups self-rising flour
pinch of salt
4 tbsp butter
4 oz/115 g sharp Cheddar cheese, grated
2 tsp chopped fresh oregano
1 egg, lightly beaten
⅔ cup milk

VARIATION

Substitute broccoli florets
for the cauliflower, or
chopped turnips for the
rutabaga, if you prefer.

Preheat the oven to 350°F/180°C. Heat the oil in a large skillet over low heat. Add the garlic and onions and cook, stirring frequently, for 5 minutes. Add the celery, rutabaga, carrots, and cauliflower and cook, stirring, for 2–3 minutes. Add the mushrooms, tomatoes, and lentils.

Put the cornstarch and water in a bowl and blend to form a smooth paste. Stir into the skillet with the stock, Tabasco sauce, and chopped oregano. Transfer to an ovenproof dish, cover with foil, and bake in the preheated oven for 20 minutes.

Meanwhile, to make the topping, sift the flour with the salt into a bowl. Add the butter and rub into the flour with your fingertips until the mixture resembles bread crumbs. Stir in most of the cheese and the chopped oregano. Beat the egg with the milk in a small bowl and add enough to the dry ingredients to make a soft dough. Turn out onto a lightly floured counter, knead briefly, then roll out to a thickness of ½ inch/1 cm. Cut into 2-inch/5-cm circles.

Remove the dish from the oven and increase the oven temperature to 400°F/200°C. Arrange the dough circles around the edge of the dish, brush with the remaining egg and milk mixture, and sprinkle with the remaining cheese. Bake for an additional 10–12 minutes. Garnish with oregano sprigs and serve.

serves 6–8 | prep 20 mins, plus 40 mins' chilling, cooling and resting | cook 40 mins

leek & spinach pie

INGREDIENTS

1 quantity puff pastry
all-purpose flour, for dusting
2 tbsp unsalted butter
2 leeks, finely sliced
5 cups fresh spinach leaves, chopped
2 eggs
1¼ cups heavy cream
pinch of dried thyme
salt and pepper

Roll out the pastry on a lightly floured counter into a rectangle about 10 x 12 inches/25 x 30 cm. Let rest for 5 minutes, then press the pastry into a 8 x 10-inch/20 x 25-cm square tart dish, leaving it overhanging the sides. Cover and let chill in the refrigerator while you make the filling.

Preheat the oven to 350°F/180°C. Melt the butter in a large skillet over medium heat. Add the leeks and cook, stirring frequently, for 5 minutes, or until softened. Add the spinach and cook for 3 minutes, stirring frequently, until wilted. Let cool.

Beat the eggs in a bowl. Stir in the cream, thyme, and salt and pepper to taste. Spread the cooked vegetables over the base of the pastry shell. Pour in the egg mixture. Put on a baking sheet and bake in the preheated oven for 30 minutes, or until set. Remove from the oven and let rest for 10 minutes before serving. Serve directly from the tart dish.

serves 6 | prep 25 mins, plus 45 mins' cooling and chilling | cook 1½ hrs

lentil, shallot & mushroom pie

INGREDIENTS
scant 1 cup Puy or green lentils
2 bay leaves
6 shallots, sliced
5 cups vegetable stock
4 tbsp butter
generous 1⅛ cups long-grain rice
8 sheets phyllo pastry, thawed if frozen
2 tbsp chopped fresh parsley
2 tsp chopped fresh fennel or savory
4 eggs, 1 beaten and 3 hard-cooked and sliced
8 oz/225 g portobello mushrooms, sliced
salt and pepper

Preheat the oven to 375°F/190°C. Put the lentils, bay leaves, and half the shallots in a large, heavy-bottom pan. Add half the stock and bring to a boil. Reduce the heat and let simmer for 25 minutes, or until the lentils are tender. Remove from the heat, season to taste with salt and pepper, and let cool completely.

Melt half the butter in a heavy-bottom pan over medium heat, add the remaining shallots, and cook, stirring frequently, for 5 minutes, or until softened. Stir in the rice and cook, stirring constantly, for 1 minute, then add the remaining stock. Season to taste with salt and pepper and bring to a boil. Reduce the heat, cover, and let simmer for 15 minutes. Remove from the heat and let cool completely.

Melt the remaining butter over low heat, then brush an ovenproof dish with a little of it. Arrange the phyllo sheets in the dish, with the sides overhanging the dish (these will make the pie lid), brushing each sheet with melted butter. Add the parsley and fennel to the rice mixture, then beat in the beaten egg. Make layers of rice, hard-cooked egg, lentils, and mushrooms in the dish, seasoning each layer to taste with salt and pepper. Bring up the phyllo sheets and scrunch into folds on top of the pie. Brush with melted butter and chill in the refrigerator for 15 minutes. Bake for 45 minutes. Let stand for 10 minutes before serving.

serves 4 | prep 20 mins | cook 1 hr 10 mins

potato-topped vegetables

INGREDIENTS

1 carrot, diced
6 oz/175 g cauliflower florets
6 oz/175 g broccoli florets
1 fennel bulb, sliced
3 oz/85 g green beans, halved
2 tbsp butter
scant ¼ cup all-purpose flour
⅔ cup vegetable stock
⅔ cup dry white wine
⅔ cup milk
6 oz/175 g cremini mushrooms, quartered
2 tbsp chopped fresh sage

TOPPING

2 lb/900 g mealy potatoes, diced
2 tbsp butter
4 tbsp plain yogurt
⅝ cup freshly grated Parmesan cheese
1 tsp fennel seeds
salt and pepper

Preheat the oven to 375°F/190°C. Bring a large pan of water to a boil, add the carrot, cauliflower, broccoli, fennel, and beans and cook for 10 minutes, or until just tender. Drain and set aside.

Melt the butter in a pan over low heat, add the flour, and cook, stirring constantly, for 1 minute. Remove from the heat and stir in the stock, wine, and milk. Return to the heat, bring to a boil and cook, stirring constantly, until thickened. Stir in the reserved vegetables, mushrooms, and sage.

To make the topping, bring a large pan of water to a boil, add the potatoes, and cook for 10–15 minutes until tender. Drain, return to the pan, and add the butter, yogurt, and half the cheese. Mash with a potato masher or a fork. Stir in the fennel seeds and salt and pepper to taste.

Spoon the vegetable mixture into a 4-cup pie dish. Top with the potato mixture. Sprinkle over the remaining cheese. Bake in the preheated oven for 30–35 minutes until golden. Serve immediately.

COOK'S TIP

For an extra creamy topping, mash the potatoes with the butter and yogurt, and before adding the cheese, beat for 1–2 minutes with a hand-held whisk.

serves 4 | prep 20 mins, plus 40 mins' chilling | cook 50 mins

cheese & vegetable pasties

INGREDIENTS

WHOLE WHEAT PIE DOUGH

1⅝ cups all-purpose whole wheat flour

pinch of salt

7 tbsp butter, diced, plus extra for greasing

4 tbsp ice-cold water

2 tbsp milk, for glazing

FILLING

2 tbsp butter

1 onion, chopped

4½ oz/125 g potatoes, chopped

3½ oz/100 g carrots, chopped

1 oz/25 g green beans, chopped

generous ⅓ cup water

2 tbsp canned and drained corn kernels

1 tbsp chopped fresh parsley

2¼ oz/60 g Cheddar cheese, grated

salt and pepper

salad greens, to serve

To make the pie dough, sift the flour with the salt into a large bowl. Add the butter and rub into the flour until the mixture resembles bread crumbs. Add the water and combine with a round-bladed knife or your fingertips to form a soft dough. Shape the dough into a ball, wrap in foil, and let chill in the refrigerator for 40 minutes.

To make the filling, melt the butter in a large pan over low heat. Add the onion, potatoes, and carrots and cook, stirring frequently, for 5 minutes. Add the beans and water. Bring to a boil, then reduce the heat and let simmer for 15 minutes. Remove from the heat and drain.

Refresh under cold running water, then drain again. Let cool.

Preheat the oven to 400°F/200°C. Grease a baking sheet. Cut the dough into quarters and roll out on a lightly floured counter into 4 circles about 6 inches/15 cm in diameter. Mix the vegetables with the corn, parsley, cheese, and salt and pepper to taste. Spoon onto one half of each pastry circle. Brush the edges with water, then fold over and press together. Transfer to the prepared baking sheet. Brush all over with milk to glaze. Bake in the preheated oven for 30 minutes until golden. Serve hot with salad greens.

serves 2 | prep 10 mins | cook 15–20 mins

cheese & tomato pizza

INGREDIENTS

1 x 10-inch/25-cm pizza dough base

TOPPING

6 tomatoes, thinly sliced

6 oz/175 g mozzarella cheese, thinly sliced

2 tbsp shredded fresh basil leaves

2 tbsp olive oil, plus extra for brushing

salt and pepper

Preheat the oven to 450°F/230°C. Brush a baking sheet with oil and put the pizza dough base on it.

To make the topping, arrange the tomato and mozzarella cheese slices alternately over the dough. Season to taste with salt and pepper, sprinkle with the basil, and drizzle with the oil.

Bake in the preheated oven for 15–20 minutes, until the crust is crisp and the cheese has melted. Serve immediately.

serves 2 | prep 25 mins | cook 35–40 mins

pizza alla siciliana

INGREDIENTS
2 x 10-inch/25-cm pizza dough bases

TOMATO SAUCE
7 oz/200 g canned chopped tomatoes
5 tbsp strained canned tomatoes
1 garlic clove, finely chopped
1 bay leaf
½ tsp dried oregano
½ tsp sugar
1 tsp balsamic vinegar
salt and pepper

TOPPING
1 eggplant, thinly sliced
2 tbsp olive oil, plus extra for brushing
6 oz/175 g mozzarella cheese, sliced
⅓ cup marinated, pitted black olives
1 tbsp capers, rinsed
4 tbsp freshly grated Parmesan cheese

Preheat the oven to 400°F/200°C. Brush 2 baking sheets with oil. To make the tomato sauce, put all the sauce ingredients in a heavy-bottom pan, and bring to a boil. Reduce the heat and let simmer, stirring occasionally, for 20 minutes, or until thickened and reduced. Remove from the heat, remove and discard the bay leaf, and let cool.

Brush the eggplant slices with the oil, then spread out on 1 prepared baking sheet. Bake in the preheated oven for 5 minutes, then turn the slices over and bake for an additional 5–10 minutes. Transfer to paper towels to drain. Increase the oven temperature to 425°F/220°C. Brush the baking sheet again with oil.

Put a pizza base on each of the prepared baking sheets and divide the tomato sauce between them, spreading it almost to the edges. Arrange the eggplant on top and cover with the mozzarella cheese. Top with olives and capers and sprinkle with Parmesan cheese. Bake for 15–20 minutes, or until golden. Serve immediately.

COOK'S TIP
For a really delicious topping, look for mozzarella di bufala—cheese made with water buffalo's milk—which has the finest flavor and texture.

VARIATION
If you like a nutty taste to your pizzas, substitute scant ¼ cup pine nuts for the capers.

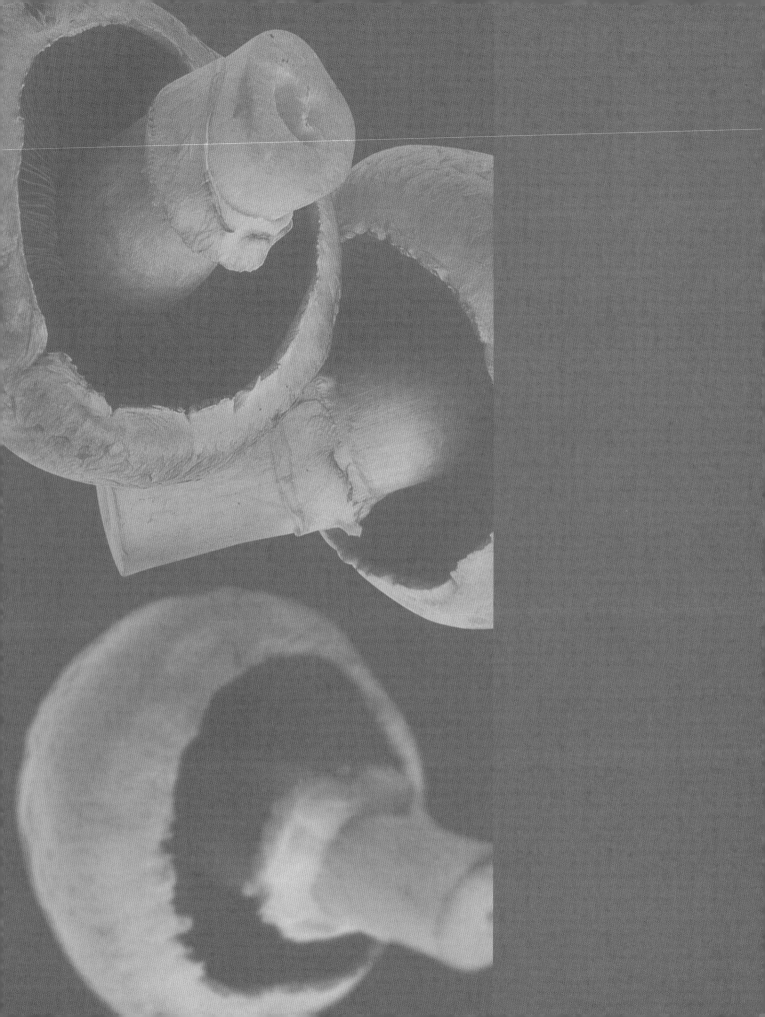

7

*There is more to side dishes than potatoes alone, but they never fail
to please, especially when cooked to crisp, golden perfection. Here
you will learn how to achieve magnificent roast potatoes every time.
You can then ring the changes with another potato special, the grated
potato cake, Rösti.*

SIDE DISHES

Discover some new ways with old favorites, such
as Brussels Sprouts with Chestnuts—ideal for
serving with a nut roast; Crispy Roast Asparagus with
olive oil and Parmesan; Green Beans with golden-toasted
Pine Nuts; and Stir-fried Broccoli with ginger. Rice is also
given a lift, with golden saffron and sweet spice or zesty
lemon grass and creamy coconut milk.

serves 6 | prep 10 mins | cook 15 mins

sautéed garlic mushrooms

INGREDIENTS

1 lb/450 g white mushrooms
5 tbsp Spanish olive oil
2 garlic cloves, finely chopped
squeeze of lemon juice
4 tbsp chopped fresh flat-leaf parsley,
   plus extra sprigs to garnish
salt and pepper
crusty bread, to serve

Wipe or brush the mushrooms clean, then trim off the stalks close to the caps. Cut any large mushrooms in half or into quarters. Heat the oil in a large, heavy-bottom skillet over medium heat, add the garlic, and cook, stirring, for 30 seconds–1 minute until lightly browned. Increase the heat to high, add the mushrooms, and cook, stirring frequently, until the mushrooms have absorbed all the oil in the skillet.

Reduce the heat to low. When the mushrooms have released their juices, increase the heat again, and cook for 4–5 minutes, stirring frequently, until the juices have almost evaporated. Add the lemon juice and season to taste with salt and pepper. Stir in the parsley and cook for another minute.

Transfer to a warmed serving dish and serve piping hot or warm, garnished with parsley sprigs. Accompany with chunks or slices of crusty bread for mopping up the cooking juices.

VARIATIONS

Wild mushrooms, such as boletuses or chanterelles, can be used in place of cultivated mushrooms. Zucchini may also be prepared in the same way, with a finely chopped small onion cooked in the oil until lightly browned before adding the garlic.

serves 4 | prep 10 mins | cook 5 mins

garlic spinach stir-fry

INGREDIENTS

6 tbsp vegetable oil

6 garlic cloves, crushed

2 tbsp black bean sauce

3 tomatoes, coarsely chopped

**2 lb/900 g spinach, tough stalks removed,
    coarsely chopped**

1 tsp chili sauce, or to taste

2 tbsp fresh lemon juice

salt and pepper

Heat the oil in a preheated wok or large skillet over high heat, add the garlic, black bean sauce, and tomatoes and stir-fry for 1 minute.

Stir in the spinach, chili sauce, and lemon juice and mix well. Cook, stirring frequently, for 3 minutes, or until the spinach is just wilted. Season to taste with salt and pepper.

Remove from the heat and serve immediately.

serves 4 | prep 10 mins | cook 6–8 mins

stir-fried broccoli

INGREDIENTS

2 tbsp vegetable oil

2 broccoli heads, cut into florets

2 tbsp soy sauce

1 tsp cornstarch

1 tbsp superfine sugar

1 tsp grated fresh gingerroot

1 garlic clove, crushed

pinch of dried red pepper flakes

1 tsp toasted sesame seeds, to garnish

Heat the oil in a large preheated wok or skillet over high heat until almost smoking. Add the broccoli and stir-fry for 4–5 minutes. Reduce the heat to medium.

Combine the soy sauce, cornstarch, sugar, ginger, garlic, and red pepper flakes in a small bowl. Add the mixture to the broccoli and cook, stirring constantly, for 2–3 minutes until the sauce thickens slightly.

Transfer to a warmed serving dish, garnish with the sesame seeds, and serve immediately.

serves 4 | prep 10 mins | cook 15–20 mins

brussels sprouts with chestnuts

INGREDIENTS
1 lb/450 g Brussels sprouts
½ cup unsalted butter
generous ¼ cup brown sugar
4 oz/115 g cooked and shelled chestnuts

Bring a large pan of salted water to a boil over high heat.

Meanwhile, trim the Brussels sprouts and remove and discard any loose outer leaves. Add to the pan of water and boil for 5–10 minutes until just tender but not too soft. Drain well, refresh under cold water, and drain again. Set aside.

Melt the butter in a heavy-bottom skillet over medium heat. Add the sugar and stir until dissolved.

Add the chestnuts and cook, stirring occasionally, until well coated and beginning to brown.

Add the sprouts to the chestnuts and mix well. Reduce the heat and cook gently, stirring occasionally, for 3–4 minutes to heat through.

Remove from the heat, transfer to a warmed serving dish, and serve immediately.

serves 4 | prep 10 mins | cook 20 mins

italian zucchini

INGREDIENTS

2 tbsp olive oil

1 large onion, chopped

1 garlic clove, finely chopped

5 zucchini, sliced

⅔ cup vegetable stock

1 tsp chopped fresh marjoram

salt and pepper

**1 tbsp chopped fresh flat-leaf parsley,
  to garnish**

Heat the oil in a large, heavy-bottom skillet over medium heat. Add the onion and garlic and cook, stirring frequently, for 5 minutes, or until softened. Add the zucchini and cook, stirring frequently, for 3–4 minutes, or until they are just beginning to brown.

Add the stock and marjoram, and season to taste with salt and pepper. Let simmer for 10 minutes, or until almost all the liquid has evaporated. Transfer to a warmed serving dish, sprinkle with the parsley, and serve immediately.

COOK'S TIP

Always leave the skin on zucchini, because this is where most of their nutrients are stored. They provide plenty of vitamin C as well as folic acid.

VARIATION

You can substitute other fresh herbs for the marjoram and parsley to bring a slightly different flavor to this dish.

serves 4 | prep 5 mins | cook 10–15 mins

crispy roast asparagus

INGREDIENTS
1 lb/450 g asparagus spears
2 tbsp extra virgin olive oil
1 tsp coarse sea salt
1 tbsp freshly grated Parmesan cheese, to serve

Preheat the oven to 400°F/200°C. Choose asparagus spears of similar widths. Trim the base of the spears so that all the stems are approximately the same length.

Arrange the asparagus in a single layer on a metal baking sheet. Drizzle with oil and sprinkle with salt.

Bake in the preheated oven for 10–15 minutes, turning once. Transfer to a warmed serving dish and serve immediately, sprinkled with the grated Parmesan cheese.

serves 4–6 | prep 20 mins | cook 50 mins–1 hr

roasted root vegetables

INGREDIENTS

3 parsnips, peeled and cut into
  2-inch/5-cm pieces
4 baby turnips, quartered
3 carrots, peeled and cut into 2-inch/5-cm pieces
1 lb/450 g butternut squash, peeled and cut into
  2-inch/5-cm chunks
1 lb/450 g sweet potato, peeled and cut into
  2-inch/5-cm chunks
2 garlic cloves, finely chopped
2 tbsp chopped fresh rosemary
2 tbsp chopped fresh thyme
2 tsp chopped fresh sage
3 tbsp olive oil
salt and pepper
2 tbsp chopped mixed fresh herbs, such as
  parsley, thyme, and mint, to garnish

Preheat the oven to 425°F/220°C. Arrange all the prepared vegetables in a single layer in a large roasting pan. Sprinkle over the garlic and herbs.

Pour over the oil and season well with salt and pepper. Toss all the ingredients together until they are well mixed and coated with the oil (you can leave them to marinate at this stage to allow the flavors to be absorbed).

Roast at the top of the preheated oven for 50 minutes–1 hour until the vegetables are cooked and browned, turning over halfway through the cooking time. Serve hot, sprinkled with mixed fresh herbs to garnish.

VARIATIONS

Shallots or wedges of red onion can be added to the root vegetables to give additional flavor and texture. Whole cloves of unpeeled garlic are also good roasted with the other vegetables. You can then squeeze out the creamy cooked garlic flesh over the roasted vegetables when eating them.

serves 6 | prep 10 mins | cook 50–55 mins

perfect roast potatoes

INGREDIENTS

3 lb/1.3 kg large, mealy potatoes, such as Idaho, Russet Burbank, or Long White, peeled and cut into even-size chunks
3 tbsp olive oil
salt

VARIATION

Small, whole, unpeeled new potatoes are delicious roasted, too. They don't need any parboiling—just coat them with the hot oil and then roast for 30–40 minutes. Drain well and season to taste with salt and pepper before serving.

Preheat the oven to 425°F/220°C. Bring a large pan of salted water to a boil, add the potatoes, and cook, covered, for 5–7 minutes. They will still be firm. Remove from the heat.

Meanwhile, add the oil to a roasting pan and heat in the preheated oven.

Drain the potatoes well and return to the pan. Cover with the lid and firmly shake the pan so that the surface of the potatoes is roughened, to help give a much crisper texture.

Remove the roasting pan from the oven and carefully tip the potatoes into the hot oil. Baste to ensure that they are all well coated with the oil.

Roast at the top of the preheated oven for 45–50 minutes until the potatoes are browned all over and thoroughly crisp, turning only once halfway through the cooking time, and basting, otherwise the crunchy edges will be destroyed.

Carefully transfer the potatoes to a warmed serving dish. Sprinkle with a little salt and serve at once. Any leftovers are delicious cold.

serves 4 | prep 15 mins | cook 1–1 ½ hours

caramelized sweet potatoes

INGREDIENTS

1 lb/450 g sweet potatoes

4 tbsp butter, plus extra for greasing

¼ cup brown sugar, maple syrup, or honey

2 tbsp orange or pineapple juice

2 oz/55 g pineapple pieces (optional)

pinch of ground cinnamon, nutmeg, or
**   allspice (optional)**

Scrub the sweet potatoes, but do not peel. Bring a large pan of salted water to a boil. Add the sweet potatoes and cook for 30–45 minutes, depending on their size, until just tender. Remove from the heat and drain well. Let cool slightly, then peel.

Preheat the oven to 400°F/200°C. Thickly slice the sweet potatoes and arrange in a single overlapping layer in a greased ovenproof dish. Cut the butter into small cubes and dot over the top.

Sprinkle with the sugar and fruit juice. Add the pineapple and spices, if using.

Bake in the preheated oven, basting occasionally, for 30–40 minutes until golden brown. Serve hot.

serves 6 | prep 10 mins | cook 20 mins

feisty potatoes

INGREDIENTS

CHILI OIL
⅔ cup olive oil
2 small fresh red chilies, split
1 tsp hot Spanish paprika

POTATOES
2 tbsp olive oil
2 lb 4 oz/1 kg potatoes, unpeeled, cut into chunks
mayonnaise, to serve

To make the chili oil, heat the oil and chilies in a heavy-bottom skillet over high heat until the chilies begin to sizzle. Remove from the heat and stir in the paprika. Set aside and let cool, then transfer the oil to a pourer with a spout. Do not strain.

Heat the olive oil in a large, heavy-bottom skillet over medium heat, add the potatoes, and cook, stirring occasionally, for 15 minutes until golden brown all over and tender. Remove with a slotted spoon and transfer to a plate covered in paper towels. Blot off the excess oil.

To serve, divide the potatoes between 6 serving plates and add a dollop of mayonnaise to each. Drizzle with the chili oil and serve warm or at room temperature. In Spain, these potatoes are traditionally served with wooden toothpicks.

serves 4 | prep 15 mins, plus 1 hr cooling and chilling | cook 30 mins

rösti

INGREDIENTS
2 lb/900 g potatoes, unpeeled
2–4 tbsp unsalted butter or vegan
  margarine
1–2 tbsp olive oil
salt and pepper

Bring a large pan of water to a boil, add the
potatoes, and cook for 10 minutes. Drain and let
cool completely. Cover and let chill in the
refrigerator for at least 30 minutes.

Peel and coarsely grate the potatoes. Melt
2 tablespoons of the butter with 1 tablespoon of
the oil in a heavy-bottom, 9-inch/23-cm skillet over
medium heat. Spread out the grated potato
evenly in the skillet, reduce the heat, and cook
for 10 minutes.

Cover the skillet with a large plate and carefully
invert the skillet and plate together so that the
potato cake drops onto the plate. Carefully slide
the potato cake back into the skillet to cook the
second side. Cook for an additional 10 minutes,
adding more butter and oil, if necessary. Season
to taste with salt and pepper and serve
immediately.

COOK'S TIP
*Chilling the parboiled
potatoes in the refrigerator
is not essential, but it will
make them easier to handle
when you grate them.*

serves 4 | prep 10 mins | cook 25–30 mins

asian coconut rice

INGREDIENTS
2 tbsp vegetable oil
1 onion, chopped
2 cups long-grain rice, rinsed and drained
1 tbsp freshly chopped lemon grass
generous 2½ cups coconut milk
1¾ cups water
6 tbsp flaked coconut, toasted

Heat the oil in a large pan over low heat, add the onion, and cook, stirring frequently, for 3 minutes. Add the rice and lemon grass and cook, stirring, for an additional 2 minutes.

Stir in the coconut milk and water and bring to a boil. Reduce the heat, cover, and let simmer for 20–25 minutes until all the liquid has been absorbed. If the rice grains have not cooked through, add a little more water and cook until tender and all the liquid has been absorbed.

Remove from the heat and add half the flaked coconut. Stir gently. Sprinkle over the remaining coconut flakes and serve.

golden rice

INGREDIENTS
1 tsp saffron threads
2 tbsp hot water
2 tbsp ghee or vegetable oil
3 onions, chopped
3 tbsp butter
1 tsp ground cumin
1 tsp ground cinnamon
1 tsp salt
½ tsp pepper
½ tsp paprika
3 bay leaves
2 cups long-grain rice, rinsed and drained
about 3½ cups vegetable stock or water
¾ cup cashew halves, toasted

Put the saffron threads and hot water into a small bowl and set aside to soak.

Meanwhile, heat the ghee in a large pan over low heat, add the onions, and cook, stirring frequently, for 5 minutes. Add the butter, cumin, cinnamon, salt, pepper, paprika, and bay leaves and cook, stirring, for 2 minutes. Add the rice and cook, stirring, for 3 minutes. Add the saffron and its soaking liquid and pour in the stock. Bring to a boil, then reduce the heat, cover, and let simmer for 20–25 minutes until all the liquid has been absorbed. If the rice grains have not cooked through, add a little more stock and cook until tender and all the liquid has been absorbed.

Remove from the heat and remove and discard the bay leaves. Taste and adjust the seasoning, if necessary. Add the cashews and stir well. Serve hot.

8

Desserts have an often well-deserved reputation for being wicked indulgences, overladen with fat, sugar, and calories. But the following recipes offer a good balance between providing a sweet treat and avoiding excess, majoring as they do on luscious fresh fruit, with the odd concession to the chocoholics.

DESSERTS

Broiled Fruit Kabobs present a fast-food feast of eye-catching exotic fruits, while spiced pears and apricots are simply left to bake in their glorious juices. More sumptuous is the all-time favorite Lemon Meringue Pie and a citrusy twist on the traditional rice pudding. Chilled temptations include the immortal Tiramisù and the aromatic Coconut & Ginger Ice Cream.

makes about 4 cups | prep 10 mins, plus 45 mins–8½ hrs' freezing and softening | no cooking required

easy mango ice cream

INGREDIENTS
2½ cups ready-made traditional custard
⅔ cup whipping cream, lightly whipped
flesh of 2 ripe mangoes, puréed
confectioners' sugar, to taste (optional)
passion fruit pulp, to serve

Mix the custard, cream, and mango purée together in a large bowl.

Taste for sweetness and, if desired, add confectioners' sugar to taste, remembering that when frozen, the mixture will taste less sweet.

Transfer to an ice-cream maker and process for 15 minutes. Alternatively, transfer the mixture to a freezerproof container. Cover and freeze for 2–3 hours until just frozen. Spoon into a bowl and beat with a fork or whisk to break down any ice crystals. Return the mixture to the container and freeze for another 2 hours. Beat the ice cream once more, then freeze for 2–3 hours until firm.

Transfer from the freezer to the refrigerator 20–30 minutes before serving to soften. Serve with the passion fruit pulp.

serves 4 | prep 10 mins, plus 1¼–9 hrs' chilling and freezing | cook 5 mins

chocolate gelato

INGREDIENTS
6 egg yolks
½ cup superfine sugar
1½ cups milk
¾ cup heavy cream
3¼ oz/90 g cooking chocolate, grated
pieces of flaked chocolate or Caraque, to decorate

Beat the egg yolks and sugar in a large, heatproof bowl until fluffy. Pour the milk, cream, and grated chocolate into a large pan and bring to a boil. Remove from the heat and whisk into the egg yolk mixture. Pour back into the pan and cook, stirring, over very low heat until thickened. Do not let it simmer. Transfer to a bowl and let cool. Cover with plastic wrap and let chill in the refrigerator for 1 hour.

Transfer to an ice-cream maker and process for 15 minutes. Alternatively, transfer the mixture to a freezerproof container. Cover and freeze for 2–3 hours until just frozen. Spoon into a bowl and beat with a fork or whisk to break down any ice crystals. Return the mixture to the container and freeze for another 2 hours. Beat the ice cream once more, then freeze for 2–3 hours until firm.

To make Caraque, melt some chocolate in a heatproof bowl set over a pan of simmering water, then spread it over an acrylic board and let set. Scrape a knife over the chocolate.

To serve, scoop the gelato into serving dishes. Decorate with flaked chocolate or Caraque.

makes about 4 cups | prep 20 mins, plus 1¼–9 hrs' cooling, freezing, and softening | cook 10 mins

coconut & ginger ice cream

INGREDIENTS

1¾ cups coconut milk
generous 1 cup whipping cream
4 egg yolks
5 tbsp superfine sugar
4 tbsp syrup from the preserved ginger
6 pieces preserved ginger, drained and chopped
2 tbsp lime juice
orange zest, to decorate

TO SERVE
litchis
ginger syrup

Heat the coconut milk and cream in a pan over medium–low heat until just beginning to simmer. Remove from the heat.

Beat the egg yolks, sugar, and ginger syrup together in a large bowl until pale and creamy. Slowly pour in the hot milk mixture, stirring constantly. Return to the pan and heat over medium–low heat, stirring constantly, until the mixture thickens and coats the back of a spoon. Remove from the heat and let cool. Stir in the ginger and lime juice.

Transfer to an ice-cream maker and process for 15 minutes. Alternatively, transfer the mixture to a freezerproof container. Cover and freeze for 2–3 hours until just frozen. Spoon into a bowl and beat with a fork or whisk to break down any ice crystals. Return the mixture to the container and freeze for another 2 hours. Beat the ice cream once more, then freeze for 2–3 hours until firm.

Transfer from the freezer to the refrigerator 20–30 minutes before serving to soften. Decorate with grated orange zest. Serve with litchis and a little ginger syrup drizzled over.

serves 4–6 | prep 10 mins, plus 1–6¾ hrs cooling, freezing, and softening | cook 5 mins

lemon sherbet with cava

INGREDIENTS
3–4 lemons
generous 1 cup water
1 cup superfine sugar
fresh mint sprigs, to garnish
1 bottle Spanish cava, chilled, to serve

Roll the lemons on the counter, pressing firmly, which helps to extract as much juice as possible. Pare off a few strips of rind and set aside for decoration, if desired, then finely grate the rind from 3 lemons. Squeeze the juice from as many of the lemons as necessary to give ¾ cup.

Put the water and sugar in a heavy-bottom pan over medium–high heat and stir to dissolve the sugar. Bring to a boil, without stirring, and boil for 2 minutes. Remove from the heat and stir in the grated lemon rind. Cover and let stand for 30 minutes, or until cool.

When the mixture is cool, stir in the lemon juice. Strain into an ice-cream maker and process according to the manufacturer's instructions. Alternatively, strain the mixture into a freezerproof container and freeze for 2 hours, or until mushy and freezing around the edges. Tip into a bowl and beat. Return to the freezer and repeat the process twice more. Remove the sherbet from the freezer 10 minutes before serving to soften.

Serve in scoops, decorated with the reserved lemon zest, if using, and mint sprigs, with a little of the cava poured over.

VARIATION
You can serve the lemon sherbet in frozen hollow lemon shells. To do this, slice the tops off 4–6 lemons and use a sharp teaspoon to scoop out the fruit. Spoon the almost-frozen sherbet into the lemons and put upright in the freezer until frozen.

serves 6 | prep 10 mins, plus 9 hrs' standing, cooling, and chilling | cook 1¼–1½ hrs

spanish caramel custard

INGREDIENTS
generous 2 cups whole milk
½ orange, with 2 pared strips of the rind
1 vanilla bean, split, or ½ tsp vanilla extract
⅞ cup superfine sugar
4 tbsp water
butter, for greasing
3 large eggs plus 2 large egg yolks

Pour the milk into a pan and add the orange rind and vanilla bean. Bring to a boil, then remove from the heat and stir in ½ cup of the sugar. Let stand for at least 30 minutes to infuse.

Meanwhile, put the remaining sugar and the water in a separate pan over medium–high heat. Stir until the sugar dissolves, then boil without stirring until the caramel turns deep golden brown.

Immediately remove the pan from the heat and squeeze in a few drops of juice from the orange to prevent further cooking. Pour into a lightly greased 5-cup soufflé dish and swirl to cover the base. Set aside.

Preheat the oven to 325°F/160°C. When the milk has infused, return the pan to the heat and bring the milk to a simmer. Beat the eggs and egg yolks together in a bowl. Pour the warm milk into the eggs, whisking constantly. Strain into the soufflé dish.

Put the soufflé dish in a roasting pan and pour in enough boiling water to come halfway up the side of the dish. Bake in the preheated oven for 1¼–1½ hours until set and a knife inserted in the center comes out clean.

Remove the soufflé dish from the roasting pan and set aside to cool completely. Cover and let chill in the refrigerator overnight.

To serve, run a metal spatula around the side of the dish, then invert onto a serving plate with a rim, shaking firmly to release.

serves 6 | prep 30 mins, plus 3½ hrs' chilling | cook 20 mins

fine chocolate tart

INGREDIENTS

CHOCOLATE PIE DOUGH

1 cup all-purpose flour, plus extra for dusting

2 tsp unsweetened cocoa, plus extra for dusting

2 tsp confectioners' sugar

pinch of salt

3½ tbsp cold butter, diced

1 egg yolk

ice-cold water

pieces of flaked white and semisweet chocolate
  or Caraque, to decorate

GANACHE FILLING

7 oz/200 g good-quality semisweet chocolate

2 tbsp unsalted butter, softened

1 cup heavy cream

1 tsp dark rum (optional)

Lightly grease a 9-inch/23-cm loose-bottom fluted tart pan. Sift the flour, cocoa, confectioners' sugar, and salt into a food processor, add the butter, and process until the mixture resembles bread crumbs. Tip the mixture into a large bowl and add the egg yolk and a little ice-cold water, just enough to bring the dough together. Turn out onto a counter dusted with extra flour and cocoa, roll out to 3¼ inches/8 cm larger than the pan, and use to line the pan. Roll the rolling pin over the pan to neaten and trim the edge. Line the tart shell with parchment paper and fill with dried beans. Chill in the refrigerator for 30 minutes. Meanwhile, preheat the oven to 375°F/190°C.

Bake the tart shell in the preheated oven for 15 minutes. Remove the paper and beans and bake for an additional 5 minutes.

To make the ganache filling, chop the chocolate and put in a heatproof bowl with the softened butter. Bring the cream to a boil in a pan, then pour over the chocolate, stirring constantly. Add the rum, if using, and continue stirring until the chocolate is completely melted. Pour into the tart shell and let chill in the refrigerator for 3 hours. Decorate with flaked chocolate or Caraque.

serves 4 | prep 15 mins | cook 10–15 mins

banana-stuffed crêpes

INGREDIENTS
scant 1⅛ cups all-purpose flour
2 tbsp brown sugar
2 eggs
2 cups milk
grated rind and juice of 1 lemon
4 tbsp butter
3 bananas
4 tbsp corn syrup

Combine the flour and sugar in a large bowl. Make a well in the center, add the eggs and half the milk to the well, and gradually beat in, drawing in the flour mixture from the sides. Beat together until smooth. Gradually beat in the remaining milk to make a smooth batter. Stir in the lemon rind.

Melt a little of the butter in an 8-inch/20-cm skillet over high heat. Pour in one-quarter of the batter. Tilt the skillet to coat the bottom and cook for 1–2 minutes until set. Flip the crêpe over and cook the second side. Slide out of the skillet and keep warm in a low oven. Repeat to make 3 more crêpes.

Slice the bananas and put in a bowl. Pour over the lemon juice to prevent discoloration. Add the syrup and toss together. Fold each crêpe into 4 and fill the center with the banana mixture. Serve warm.

serves 4 | prep 10 mins, plus 10 mins' marinating | cook 10 mins

broiled fruit kabobs

INGREDIENTS

2 tbsp hazelnut oil

2 tbsp honey

juice and finely grated rind of 1 lime

2 pineapple rings, halved

8 strawberries

1 pear, peeled, cored, and thickly sliced

1 banana, peeled and thickly sliced

2 kiwifruit, peeled and quartered

1 carambola, cut into 4 slices

Preheat the broiler to medium. Mix the oil, honey, and lime juice and rind together in a large, shallow, nonmetallic dish. Add the fruit and turn to coat. Cover and let marinate for 10 minutes.

Thread the fruit alternately onto 4 long metal skewers, beginning with a piece of pineapple and ending with a slice of carambola.

Brush the kabobs with the marinade and cook under the broiler, brushing frequently with the marinade, for 5 minutes. Turn the kabobs over, brush with the remaining marinade, and broil for an additional 5 minutes. Serve immediately.

COOK'S TIP

Honey varies widely in flavor and the best quality, with a distinctive taste, is usually made from a single type of blossom. For this recipe, try orange blossom, acacia, or lime flower.

VARIATION

You can use other types of fruit for these kabobs, such as seedless grapes, mango slices, and papaya chunks.

serves 4 | prep 5 mins | cook 30 mins

spiced baked pears

INGREDIENTS
4 large, firm eating pears
⅔ cup apple juice
1 cinnamon stick
4 whole cloves
1 bay leaf

Preheat the oven to 350°F/180°C.

Peel and core the pears, then quarter. Put in an ovenproof dish and add the remaining ingredients.

Cover the dish and bake in the preheated oven for 30 minutes.

Serve the pears hot or cold.

serves 4 | prep 10 mins | cook 12–15 mins

baked apricots with honey

INGREDIENTS
butter, for greasing
4 apricots, halved and pitted
4 tbsp slivered almonds
4 tbsp honey
pinch of ground ginger or grated nutmeg
vanilla ice cream, to serve (optional)

Preheat the oven to 400°F/200°C. Lightly grease an ovenproof dish large enough to hold the apricot halves in a single layer.

Arrange the apricot halves in the dish, cut-sides up. Sprinkle with the almonds and drizzle over the honey. Dust with the spice.

Bake in the preheated oven for 12–15 minutes until the apricots are tender and the almonds golden. Remove from the oven and serve immediately, with ice cream on the side, if desired.

serves 6 | prep 15 mins | cook 25–30 mins

rhubarb crumble

INGREDIENTS
2 lb/900 g rhubarb
generous ½ cup superfine sugar
grated rind and juice of 1 orange
cream, yogurt, or custard, to serve

CRUMBLE
scant 1⅝ cups all-purpose or whole wheat flour
½ cup butter
generous ½ cup packed brown sugar
1 tsp ground ginger

Preheat the oven to 375°F/190°C.

Cut the rhubarb into 1-inch/2.5-cm lengths and put in a 7¼-cup ovenproof dish with the sugar and orange rind and juice.

To make the crumble, put the flour in a bowl, add the butter, and rub into the flour with your fingertips until the mixture resembles bread crumbs. Stir in the sugar and ginger.

Spread the crumble evenly over the fruit and press down lightly with a fork.

Put on a baking sheet. Bake in the center of the preheated oven for 25–30 minutes until the crumble is golden brown.

Serve warm with cream, yogurt, or custard.

serves 4–6 | prep 10 mins | cook 30 minutes

rice pudding

INGREDIENTS
1 large orange
1 lemon
4 cups milk
scant 1¼ cups Spanish short-grain rice
generous ½ cup superfine sugar
1 vanilla bean, split
pinch of salt
½ cup heavy cream
brown sugar, to serve (optional)

Finely grate the rinds from the orange and lemon and set aside. Rinse a heavy-bottom pan with cold water, but do not dry it.

Put the milk and rice in the pan over medium–high heat and bring to a boil. Reduce the heat, stir in the superfine sugar, vanilla bean, orange and lemon rinds, and salt and let simmer, stirring frequently, until the pudding is thick and creamy and the rice grains are tender. This can take up to 30 minutes, depending on how wide the pan is.

Remove the vanilla bean and stir in the cream. Serve immediately, sprinkled with brown sugar, if desired, or let cool completely, cover, and let chill until required. (The pudding will thicken as it cools, so stir in extra milk, if necessary.)

serves 4 | prep 20 mins, plus 2 hrs' chilling | no cooking required

tiramisù

INGREDIENTS

scant 1 cup strong black coffee,
 cooled to room temperature
4 tbsp orange liqueur, such as Cointreau
3 tbsp orange juice
16 Italian ladyfingers
1⅛ cups mascarpone cheese
1¼ cups heavy cream, lightly whipped
3 tbsp confectioners' sugar
grated rind of 1 orange
2¼ oz/60 g chocolate, grated

TO DECORATE
chopped toasted almonds
candied orange peel

Pour the cooled coffee into a pitcher and stir in the orange liqueur and orange juice. Put half the ladyfingers in the base of a serving dish, then pour over half the coffee mixture.

Put the mascarpone cheese in a separate bowl with the cream, confectioners' sugar, and orange rind and mix well together. Spread half the mascarpone mixture over the coffee-soaked ladyfingers, then arrange the remaining ladyfingers on top. Pour over the remaining coffee mixture and then spread over the remaining mascarpone mixture. Sprinkle over the grated chocolate.

Chill in the refrigerator for at least 2 hours. Serve decorated with chopped toasted almonds and candied orange peel.

serves 6 | prep 30 mins, plus 1 ½ hrs' chilling | cook 1 ½ hrs

toffee apple tart

INGREDIENTS
butter, for greasing
all-purpose flour, for dusting
1 quantity rich shortcrust pie dough, chilled
heavy cream to serve

FILLING
3 lb/1.3 kg Cox's Orange Pippin or other firm,
  sweet apples, peeled and cored
1 tsp lemon juice
3½ tbsp butter
½ cup superfine sugar
1 cup granulated sugar
⅓ cup cold water
⅔ cup heavy cream
confectioners' sugar, for dusting (optional)

Lightly grease a 9-inch/23-cm loose-bottom fluted tart pan. Roll out the dough on a lightly floured counter and use to line the pan. Roll the rolling pin over the pan to neaten and trim the edge. Line with parchment paper and fill with dried beans. Chill in the refrigerator for 30 minutes. Meanwhile, preheat the oven to 375°F/190°C.

Bake the tart shell in the preheated oven for 10 minutes. Remove the paper and beans. Bake for an additional 5 minutes.

Meanwhile, take 4 apples, cut each one into 8 pieces and toss in the lemon juice to prevent discoloration. Melt the butter in a skillet over medium heat, add the apple pieces, and cook until just beginning to caramelize on the edges. Remove from the pan and let cool.

Thinly slice the remaining apples, put them in a pan with the superfine sugar and cook for 20–30 minutes until soft. Spoon the cooked apple slices into the tart shell and arrange the reserved apple pieces on top in a circle. Bake for 30 minutes.

Put the granulated sugar and water in a pan and heat until the sugar dissolves. Boil until caramelized. Remove from the heat and add the cream, stirring constantly to make a toffee. Remove the tart from the oven, pour the toffee over the apples, and chill in the refrigerator for 1 hour. When ready to serve, sift confectioners' sugar over the tart, if desired. Serve with cream.

serves 8–10 | prep 30 mins, plus 45 mins' chilling | cook 50 mins

lemon meringue pie

INGREDIENTS
butter, for greasing
1 quantity rich shortcrust pie dough, chilled
all-purpose flour, for dusting
3 tbsp cornstarch
generous ⅓ cup superfine sugar
grated rind of 3 lemons
1¼ cups cold water
⅔ cup lemon juice
3 egg yolks
4 tbsp unsalted butter, diced

MERINGUE
3 egg whites
generous ¾ cup superfine sugar
1 tsp golden granulated sugar

Grease a 10-inch/25-cm fluted tart pan. Roll out the pie dough on a lightly floured counter to a circle 2 inches/5 cm larger than the tart pan and use to line the pan. Roll the rolling pin over the pan to neaten and trim the edge. Prick the base of the tart shell with a fork and let chill, uncovered, in the refrigerator for 20–30 minutes.

Preheat the oven to 400°F/ 200°C. Preheat a baking sheet. Line the pastry shell with parchment paper and fill with dried beans. Put on the preheated baking sheet and bake in the preheated oven for 15 minutes. Remove the paper and beans and bake for an additional 10 minutes until the dough is dry and just coloring. Remove from the oven and reduce the oven temperature to 300°F/150°C.

Put the cornstarch, sugar, and lemon rind in a pan. Pour in a little of the water and blend to a smooth paste. Gradually add the remaining water and the lemon juice. Put the pan over medium heat and bring the mixture to a boil, stirring constantly. Reduce the heat and let simmer gently for 1 minute until smooth and glossy. Remove from the heat. Beat in the egg yolks, one at a time, then beat in the butter. Put the pan in a bowl of cold water to cool the filling. When cool, spoon the mixture into the pastry shell.

To make the meringue, whisk the egg whites using an electric mixer until thick and soft peaks form. Gradually add the superfine sugar, whisking well after each addition. The mixture should be glossy and firm. Spoon the meringue over the filling to cover it completely and make a seal with the pastry shell. Swirl the meringue into peaks and sprinkle with the granulated sugar.

Bake for 20–30 minutes until the meringue is crisp and pale gold (the center should still be soft). Let cool slightly before serving.

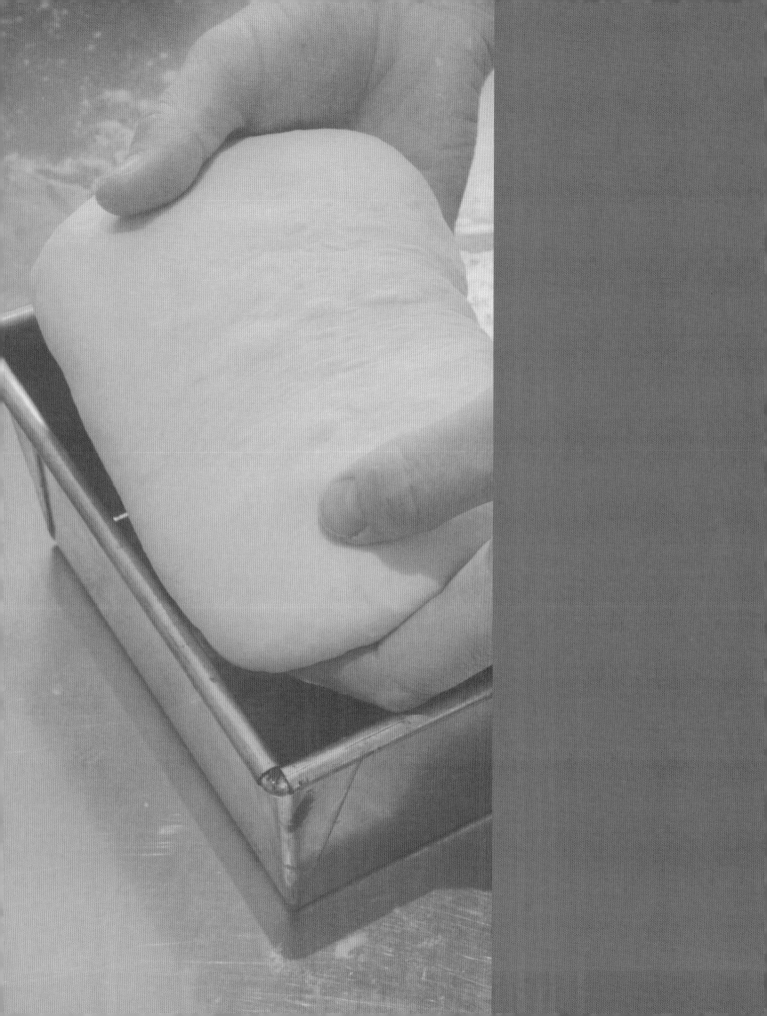

9

Freshly baked bread, with its heavenly aroma and taste, has to be one of the best, and simplest, eating pleasures, and these basic, no-nonsense recipes are sure to give you both the inspiration and the confidence to make your own delicious loaves. You really can achieve great results with minimal effort!

BREADS, CAKES & COOKIES

You may, however, be more inclined to put your baking efforts into the sweet rather than the savory, but the rewards will be equally satisfying. Featured are the great cake classics, such as the decorative Coffee & Walnut Cake and the dense Rich Chocolate Cake, while other teatime treats include dainty Almond Cookies and chewy Hazelnut & Almond Oaties.

makes 1 large loaf or 8 baps | prep 20 mins, plus 1½ hrs' proving | cook 15–30 mins

fresh bread

INGREDIENTS
butter, for greasing
1 lb/450 g white bread flour, plus extra
for dusting
1 tsp salt
1 x ⅛ oz/7 g sachet active dry yeast
1 tbsp vegetable oil or melted butter
1½ cups tepid water

Grease a 2-lb/900-g loaf pan or 2 baking sheets.

Mix the flour, salt, and yeast together in a large bowl. Make a well in the center, add the oil and water to the well, and gradually mix in, drawing in the flour mixture from the sides, to form a soft dough.

Use a free-standing electric mixer to knead the dough with the dough hook for 4–5 minutes. Alternatively, turn the dough out onto a lightly floured counter and knead well for 5–7 minutes. The dough should have a smooth appearance and feel elastic.

Return the dough to the bowl, cover with plastic wrap, and leave in a warm place to rise for 1 hour, or until the dough has doubled in size.

Turn out onto the counter and knead again until smooth. For a loaf shape, shape as a rectangle the length of the loaf pan and 3 times the width. Fold the dough into 3 and put into the prepared pan with the join underneath so that you have a well-shaped loaf. Alternatively, divide the dough into 8 equal pieces, shape into circles, and space well apart on the prepared baking sheets. Dust with a little extra flour for a softer crust. Cover with plastic wrap and let rise again in a warm place for 30 minutes, or until the loaf is well risen above the pan or the baps are doubled in size.

Meanwhile, preheat the oven to 450°F/230°C. If baking a loaf, bake in the center of the preheated oven for 25–30 minutes until cooked through—it should sound hollow when tapped on the bottom. If the top is getting too brown, reduce the temperature a little. For the baps, bake for 15–20 minutes, swapping the baking sheets around halfway through the cooking time. Transfer to wire racks to cool. Eat the bread as fresh as possible.

makes 2 small loaves | prep 20 mins, plus 2¼ hrs' proving | cook 40 mins

olive & sun-dried tomato bread

INGREDIENTS

2¾ cups all-purpose flour, plus extra for dusting

1 tsp salt

1 x ⅛ oz/7 g sachet active dry yeast

1 tsp brown sugar

1 tbsp chopped fresh thyme

4 tbsp olive oil, plus extra for oiling

scant 1 cup warm water (heated to 122°F/50°C)

⅓ cup black olives, pitted and sliced

⅓ cup green olives, pitted and sliced

generous ⅓ cup sun-dried tomatoes in olive oil, drained and sliced

1 egg yolk, beaten

Mix the flour, salt, and yeast together in a large bowl, then stir in the sugar and thyme. Make a well in the center, add most of the oil and water to the well, and gradually mix in, drawing in the flour mixture from the sides, to form a soft dough. Add the remaining oil and water, if necessary. Mix in the olives and sun-dried tomatoes. Turn the dough out onto a lightly floured counter and knead well for 5 minutes, then shape into a ball. Brush the bowl with oil and return the dough to the bowl. Cover with plastic wrap and leave in a warm place to rise for 1½ hours, or until the dough has doubled in size.

Dust a baking sheet with flour. Turn the dough out on the counter and knead lightly again. Cut in half and shape each half into an oval or circle. Put on the prepared baking sheet, cover with plastic wrap, and let rise again in a warm place for 45 minutes, or until doubled in size.

Meanwhile, preheat the oven to 400°F/200°C. Make 3 shallow, diagonal cuts in the top of each piece of dough. Brush with the egg. Bake in the preheated oven for 40 minutes, or until cooked through—they should be golden on top and sound hollow when tapped on the bottom. Transfer to wire racks to cool. Store in an airtight container for up to 3 days.

irish soda bread

INGREDIENTS
butter, for greasing
1 lb/450 g all-purpose flour, plus extra for dusting
1 tsp salt
1 tsp baking soda
1¾ cups buttermilk

Preheat the oven to 425°F/220°C. Grease a baking sheet.

Sift the flour, salt, and baking soda into a large bowl. Make a well in the center, add most of the buttermilk to the well, and gradually mix in, drawing in the flour mixture from the sides, to form a very soft but not too wet dough. Add the remaining buttermilk, if necessary.

Turn the dough out onto a lightly floured counter and knead lightly. Shape into an 8-inch/20-cm circle.

Put the dough on the prepared baking sheet, cut a cross in the top and bake in the preheated oven for 25–30 minutes until cooked through—it should sound hollow when tapped on the bottom. Eat while still warm. Soda bread is always best eaten the same day as it is made.

VARIATIONS
Add 1 tablespoon chopped fresh rosemary and 1/3 cup golden raisins. For a change, make with whole wheat flour and add a handful of seeds or coarse oatmeal, or make with half stoneground flour and half white flour and 3/8 cup chopped walnuts. Sweet soda bread can be made with the addition of 1/8 cup sugar and 1/2 cup mixed dried fruits. This is known as "spotted dog." Another sweet version can be made with the addition of 1 tablespoon sugar and 3 oz/85 g coarsely chopped semisweet chocolate.

makes 8 | prep 25 mins, plus 1 hr 40 mins standing and proving | cook 10 mins

naan breads

INGREDIENTS
1 tsp fresh yeast
about ⅔ cup warm water
1 tsp sugar
1 cup all-purpose flour, plus extra for dusting
1 tsp salt
3 tbsp ghee or vegetable oil
1 tsp chili powder
½ tsp ground coriander

Mix the yeast, water, and sugar together in a bowl and let stand for 10 minutes.

Sift the flour with the salt into a separate bowl. Make a well in the center, add 1 tablespoon of the ghee and the yeast mixture to the well, and gradually mix in, drawing in the flour from the sides, to form a smooth dough. Shape into a ball. Turn out onto a lightly floured counter. Knead for 5 minutes. Return to the bowl, cover, and leave in a warm place to rise for 1½ hours, or until doubled in size.

Knead the dough again for 3 minutes. Divide into 8 pieces and shape each piece into a ball. Flatten into ovals ¼ inch/5 mm thick. Mix the chili powder and coriander together, then turn the naan breads in the spice mixture until evenly coated.

Preheat the broiler to high. Line a broiler rack with foil and brush with ghee. Arrange the naans on top and brush with ghee. Cook under the broiler for 10 minutes, turning and brushing with the remaining ghee. Serve hot.

biscuits

INGREDIENTS
1 lb/450 g all-purpose flour, plus extra for dusting
½ tsp salt
2 tsp baking powder
4 tbsp butter
2 tbsp superfine sugar
generous 1 cup milk, plus extra for glazing
strawberry preserve and clotted cream, to serve

Preheat the oven to 425°F/220°C. Sift the flour, salt, and baking powder into a bowl. Add the butter and rub into the flour mixture with your fingertips until the mixture resembles bread crumbs. Stir in the sugar.

Make a well in the center, add the milk to the well, and gradually stir in with a round-bladed knife to form a soft dough.

Turn out the dough onto a lightly floured counter and lightly flatten until it is of an even thickness, about ½ inch/1 cm. Don't be heavy-handed—biscuits need a light touch.

Use a 2½-inch/6-cm pastry cutter to cut out the biscuits and put on a baking sheet.

Brush with a little milk to glaze. Bake in the preheated oven for 10–12 minutes until golden and well risen.

Transfer to a wire rack to cool. Serve freshly baked with the traditional accompaniments of strawberry preserve and clotted cream.

VARIATIONS
To make fruit biscuits, add ¹/₃ cup mixed fruit with the sugar. To make whole wheat biscuits, use whole wheat flour and omit the sugar. These are delicious served with soup or as an accompaniment to cheese. To make cheese biscuits, omit the sugar and fruit and add ¹/₂ cup finely grated Cheddar or Double Gloucester cheese to the mixture with 1 teaspoon of dry mustard powder.

makes 6 bars | prep 20 mins, plus 40 mins' cooling | cook 55 mins

carrot cake

INGREDIENTS
butter, for greasing
¾ cup self-rising flour
pinch of salt
1 tsp ground allspice
½ tsp ground nutmeg
generous ⅝ cup packed brown sugar
2 eggs, beaten
5 tbsp sunflower-seed or corn oil
4½ oz/125 g carrots, peeled and grated
1 banana, chopped
generous ⅛ cup chopped toasted mixed nuts

FROSTING
3 tbsp butter, softened
3 tbsp cream cheese
1½ cups confectioners' sugar, sifted
1 tsp fresh orange juice
grated rind of ½ orange
walnut halves or pieces, to decorate

Preheat the oven to 375°F/190°C. Grease a 7-inch/18-cm square cake pan and line with parchment paper.

Sift the flour, salt, allspice, and nutmeg into a bowl. Stir in the brown sugar, then stir in the eggs and oil. Add the carrots, banana, and nuts and mix well together.

Spoon the batter into the prepared pan and level the surface. Bake in the preheated oven for 55 minutes, or until golden and just firm to the touch. Let cool slightly. When cool enough to handle, turn out onto a wire rack, and let cool completely.

To make the frosting, put the butter, cream cheese, confectioners' sugar, and orange juice and rind in a bowl and beat together until creamy. Spread the frosting over the top of the cake, then use a fork to make shallow, wavy lines in the frosting. Sprinkle over the walnuts, cut the cake into bars, and serve.

makes 10–12 slices | prep 25 mins, plus 40 mins' soaking and cooling | cook 45 mins

rich chocolate cake

INGREDIENTS

scant ⅔ cup raisins
finely grated rind and juice of 1 orange
¾ cup butter, diced, plus extra for greasing
3½ oz/100 g semisweet chocolate, at least 70%
  cocoa solids, broken into pieces
4 large eggs, beaten
½ cup superfine sugar
1 tsp vanilla extract
scant ½ cup all-purpose flour
generous ½ cup ground almonds
½ tsp baking powder
pinch of salt
⅓ cup blanched almonds, lightly toasted
  and chopped
confectioners' sugar, sifted, to decorate

Preheat the oven to 350°F/180°C. Line a deep, loose-bottom, 10-inch/25-cm round cake pan with waxed paper. Grease the paper.

Put the raisins in a small bowl, add the orange juice, and let soak for 20 minutes.

Melt the butter and chocolate together in a small pan over medium heat, stirring. Remove from the heat and set aside to cool.

Using an electric mixer, beat the eggs, sugar, and vanilla essence together for 3 minutes, or until light and fluffy. Stir in the cooled chocolate mixture.

Drain the raisins if they have not absorbed all the orange juice. Sift the flour, ground almonds, baking powder, and salt into the egg and sugar mixture. Add the raisins, orange rind, and almonds and fold all the ingredients together.

Spoon into the cake pan and level the surface. Bake in the preheated oven for 40 minutes, or until a toothpick inserted into the center comes out clean and the cake starts to come away from the side of the pan. Let cool in the pan for 10 minutes, then remove from the pan, transfer to a wire rack, and let cool completely. Dust the surface with confectioners' sugar before serving.

serves 4 | prep 20 mins, plus 2½ hrs' cooling and chilling | cook 1 hr

coffee & walnut cake

INGREDIENTS

FROSTING

6 tbsp organic unsweetened cocoa

2 tbsp cornstarch

6 tbsp superfine sugar

½ cup strong black coffee, cooled

generous 1 cup milk

SPONGE

scant 2 cups all-purpose flour

1 tbsp baking powder

scant ½ cup sugar

6 tbsp butter, softened, plus extra for greasing

2 eggs

⅔ cup milk

3 tbsp hot strong black coffee

generous ½ cup walnuts, chopped

⅓ cup golden raisins

walnut halves, to decorate

To make the frosting, put all the frosting ingredients into a blender or food processor and process until creamy. Transfer to a pan and heat, stirring, over medium heat until bubbling. Cook for 1 minute, then pour into a heatproof bowl. Let cool, then cover with plastic wrap, and let chill in the refrigerator for at least 2 hours.

Preheat the oven to 375°F/190°C. Grease a 9-inch/23-cm loose-bottom cake pan and line with parchment paper. To make the sponge, sift the flour with the baking powder into a bowl, then stir in the sugar. In a separate bowl, beat the butter, eggs, milk, and coffee together, then mix into the flour mixture. Stir in the chopped walnuts and the golden raisins. Spoon into the prepared cake pan and level the surface. Bake in the preheated oven for 1 hour. Let cool slightly. When cool enough to handle, turn out onto a wire rack, and let cool completely. Spread the frosting over the top of the cold cake, decorate with the walnut halves, and serve.

makes 12–18 pieces | prep 15 mins, plus 15 mins' cooling | cook 1 hr 35 mins

gingerbread

INGREDIENTS
1 lb/450 g all-purpose flour
3 tsp baking powder
1 tsp baking soda
3 tsp ground ginger
¾ cup butter
⅞ cup packed brown sugar
½ cup molasses
½ cup corn syrup, plus extra
  to serve (optional)
1 egg, beaten
1¼ cups milk
cream, to serve (optional)

Preheat the oven to 325°F/160°C. Line a 9-inch/23-cm square cake pan, 2 inches/5 cm deep, with waxed paper or parchment paper.

Sift the dry ingredients into a large bowl.

Put the butter, sugar, molasses, and syrup in a medium pan over low heat and heat until the butter has melted and the sugar has dissolved. Let cool a little. Mix the beaten egg with the milk and add to the cooled syrup mixture.

Add all the liquid ingredients to the flour mixture and beat well using a wooden spoon until the mixture is smooth and glossy.

Pour the batter into the prepared pan and bake in the center of the preheated oven for 1½ hours until well risen, just firm to the touch, and a skewer inserted into the center of the cake comes out clean. This gives a lovely sticky gingerbread, but

if you prefer a firmer cake, bake for an additional 15 minutes.

Remove from the oven and let the cake cool in the pan. When cool, remove the cake from the pan with the lining paper. Wrap in foil and store in an airtight container for up to 1 week to allow the flavors to mature.

Cut into wedges and serve for tea or serve with cream as a dessert. Extra warmed syrup is an added indulgence.

makes 30 | prep 15 mins | cook 10 mins

orange cream cheese cookies

INGREDIENTS

1 cup butter or margarine,
 plus extra for greasing
1 cup packed brown sugar
⅜ cup cream cheese
1 egg, lightly beaten
generous 2⅓ cups all-purpose flour
1 tsp baking soda
1 tbsp fresh orange juice
1 tsp finely grated orange rind, plus extra
 for decorating
raw brown sugar, for sprinkling

Preheat the oven to 375°F/190°C. Grease a large baking sheet.

Put the butter, sugar, and cream cheese in a large bowl and beat until light and fluffy. Beat in the egg. Sift in the flour and baking soda and add the orange juice and rind. Mix well.

Drop about 30 rounded tablespoonfuls of the batter onto the prepared baking sheet, making sure that they are well spaced. Sprinkle with the raw brown sugar.

Bake in the preheated oven for 10 minutes, or until the cookies are light brown at the edges.

Let cool on a wire rack. Decorate with orange rind before serving.

makes 36 | prep 10 mins | cook 12 mins

hazelnut & almond oaties

INGREDIENTS

**¾ cup butter or margarine, plus extra
  for greasing**
¾ cup raw brown sugar
1 egg
scant ¾ cup all-purpose flour
½ tsp salt
1 tsp baking soda
¼ tsp almond extract
1½ cups rolled oats
scant ¼ cup hazelnuts, coarsely chopped
scant ¼ cup almonds, coarsely chopped
1 cup semisweet chocolate chips

Preheat the oven to 375°F/190°C. Grease 1 or more large baking sheets.

Put the butter and sugar in a large bowl and beat until light and fluffy. Beat in the egg.

Sift the flour, salt, and baking soda into a separate bowl, then stir into the butter mixture.

Add the almond extract and oats and beat thoroughly. Stir in the nuts and chocolate chips.

Divide small teaspoonfuls of the batter between the prepared baking sheets, making sure that they are well spaced. Bake in the preheated oven for 12 minutes, or until the oaties are golden brown. Let cool on a wire rack before serving.

makes 60 | prep 15 minutes | cook 15–20 minutes

almond cookies

INGREDIENTS

11 tbsp butter, at room temperature,
  plus extra for greasing
generous ¾ cup superfine sugar
generous ¾ cup all-purpose flour
generous ¼ cup ground almonds
pinch of salt
½ cup blanched almonds, lightly toasted and
  finely chopped
finely grated rind of 1 large lemon
4 egg whites

Preheat the oven to 350°F/180°C. Grease 1 or more baking sheets. Put the butter and sugar into a bowl and beat until light and fluffy. Sift in the flour, ground almonds, and salt, tipping in any ground almonds left in the strainer. Use a large metal spoon to fold in the chopped almonds and lemon rind.

Whisk the egg whites in a separate clean, greasefree bowl until soft peaks form. Fold the egg whites into the almond mixture.

Drop small teaspoonfuls of the batter onto the prepared baking sheet, making sure that they are well spaced. (You may need to bake in batches.) Bake in the preheated oven for 15–20 minutes until golden brown at the edges. Let cool on a wire rack before serving.

makes 24 | prep 10 mins, plus 30 mins' chilling | cook 12 mins

nutty chocolate drizzles

INGREDIENTS
1 cup butter or margarine, plus extra for greasing
generous 1⅓ cups raw brown sugar
1 egg
1 cup all-purpose flour, sifted
1 tsp baking powder
1 tsp baking soda
1½ cups rolled oats
⅜ cup bran
⅜ cup wheat germ
¾ cup mixed nuts, toasted and coarsely chopped
¾ cup semisweet chocolate chips
½ cup raisins and golden raisins
6 oz/175 g semisweet chocolate,
  coarsely chopped

Preheat the oven to 350°F/180°C. Grease a large baking sheet. Put the butter, sugar, and egg in a large bowl and beat until light and fluffy. Add the flour, baking powder, baking soda, oats, bran, and wheat germ and mix together until well combined. Stir in the nuts, chocolate chips, and dried fruit.

Put 24 rounded tablespoonfuls of the batter onto the prepared baking sheet. Bake in the preheated oven for 12 minutes, or until golden brown.

Let cool on a wire rack. Meanwhile, put the chocolate pieces in a heatproof bowl set over a pan of gently simmering water and heat until melted. Stir the chocolate, then let cool slightly. Use a spoon to drizzle the chocolate in waves over the cookies, or spoon into a pastry bag and pipe zig-zag lines over the cookies. Chill in an airtight container in the refrigerator for 30 minutes before serving.

makes 30 | prep 15 mins, plus 30 mins' chilling | cook 15 mins

chocolate & brazil nut crunchies

INGREDIENTS
4 tbsp butter or margarine, plus extra
  for greasing
4 tbsp white vegetable fat
scant ¾ cup raw brown sugar
1 egg
1 tsp vanilla extract
1 tbsp milk
scant ¾ cup all-purpose flour, unsifted
1⅛ cups rolled oats
1 tsp baking soda
pinch of salt
1 cup semisweet chocolate chips
scant ¼ cup Brazil nuts, chopped

Put the butter, fat, sugar, egg, vanilla extract, and milk in a blender or food processor and process for at least 3 minutes until a fluffy consistency is reached.

Mix the flour, oats, baking soda, and salt together in a large bowl. Stir in the egg mixture, then the chocolate chips and nuts, and mix well together. Cover the bowl with plastic wrap and let chill in the refrigerator for 30 minutes until firm.

Meanwhile, preheat the oven to 350°F/180°C. Grease a large baking sheet.

Put 30 rounded tablespoonfuls of the batter onto the prepared baking sheet, making sure that they are well spaced. Bake in the preheated oven for 15 minutes, or until golden brown.

Let cool on a wire rack before serving.

Index